Ask the
dog Keeper

MARC MORRONE
with Amy Fernandez

I dedicate this book to the memory of Paw Paw—Martha Stewart's Chow whom I had the pleasure of working with for ten years.

In his own good-natured and humble way, he achieved more canine milestones than any other dog I ever knew—be it as canine father, TV star, Westminster winner, or just household pet, he performed all his duties with a canine smile and a wagging tail.

Original Illustrations © 2009 by Jason O'Malley. Photographs © 2009 by Mary Bloom, Tara Darling, and Isabelle Français.

Library of Congress Cataloging-in-Publication Data

Morrone, Marc, 1960-
  [Ask the dog keeper]
  Marc Morrone's ask the dog keeper / by Marc Morrone with Amy Fernandez.
      p. cm.
  ISBN 978-1-933958-29-3
  1. Dogs—Miscellanea. 2. Dogs—Health—Miscellanea. 3. Dogs—Behavior—Miscellanea. I.
Fernandez, Amy. II. Title. III. Title: Ask the dog keeper.
  SF427.M77 2009
  636.7—dc22
                              200900982

A Division of BowTie, Inc.
3 Burroughs
Irvine, California, 92618

Printed and bound in Singapore
16 15 14 13 12 11 10 09   1 2 3 4 5 6 7 8 9 10

CONTENTS

Foreword by Martha Stewart 4

Introduction 7

Food 11
Q&A ON FEEDING, NUTRITION, AND DIETS

Poop 21
Q&A ON HOUSE-TRAINING, ACCIDENTS, AND PECULIAR POTTY BEHAVIOR

School 33
Q&A ON TRICKS, TRAINING, AND BEHAVIOR ISSUES

Health 47
Q&A ON VACCINATIONS, VITAMINS, AND VETS

Habits 59
Q&A ON ODD TENDENCIES, SPECIAL ABILITIES, AND MORE

True or False? 71
Q&A ON BASIC DOGGY MYTHS, MISNOMERS, AND URBAN LEGENDS

Body 83
Q&A ON CANINE ANATOMY AND BREED CHARACTERISTICS

Care 101
Q&A ON COHABITATION AND HUSBANDRY

Friends 117
Q&A ON INTERACTION WITH PEOPLE AND OTHER ANIMALS

FOREWORD

BY MARTHA STEWART

I have owned dogs since 1969, when we bought a beautiful Keeshond female from a breeder in Litchfield, Connecticut.

Growing up in a family of eight in Nutley, New Jersey, I had one unfortunate experience with dog ownership that is still painful for me to remember. A Fox Terrier named Shiner was brought home by our father, but, untrained and unruly, he was quickly given back by our mother, who could not cope with six little children and a dog. I have never forgotten the little guy's forlorn look at me when I went to visit him shortly after he was returned, and I vowed to get my own dog when I had my own house and promised to love it and train it and nurture it well.

Little Bear, the Keeshond, was a charming and very special dog. Bred as working dogs by the barge owners on the canals of Holland, these fluffy, pretty, smart, very trainable dogs are devoted to guarding quietly, rescuing those in trouble, and being benign and perfect companions for old and young alike. We adored Little Bear, bred her once, and raised her nine healthy pups, all of whom were named "*something* Bear."

She lived with us until she died simply of old age at seventeen. While I still had Little Bear, I saw another dog that appealed to me—a large, manly, fluffy-coated Chow Chow. I did a bit of research and, soon after the demise of Little Bear, located Harry the Chow in northwestern Connecticut at a very nice breeding kennel.

We loved the Chow Chow breed from day one. Quiet, regal, non-obsequious, intensely loyal and fun, this ancient Chinese breed fit our lifestyle and our home. We have had several more wonderful Chows since Harry—Blue Maxmillian, Zuleika Dobson I and Zuleika Dobson II (Zuzu), Chin Chin, Empress Wu, and Paw Paw, our last Chow Chow. Each of these Chows was special and wonderful, and all lived good long lives (about fourteen years) as honored members of our family, except for Wu, who had a series of unsolvable problems. We have cherished these dogs, photographed them, and introduced them to our friends and colleagues in our books and magazines as well as on my television show. Everyone loved the Chows, and I am now waiting for a dog to take Paw Paw's place as the "king" of my houses. Four years ago, as Paw Paw aged, I bought two very different dogs to keep him company—two female French Bulldogs, Francesca and Sharkey.

These dogs took me completely by surprise—they demanded attention, wanted a wardrobe of coats and sweaters, and wanted comfy beds to lounge in during the day but a place in my bed, under the covers, at night. Unlike the Chows, these girls have extraordinary energy, run miles a day, ingratiate themselves into every situation, and even watch television. Like the Chows, they also love to pose for pictures and act on television, and they do not mind at all working ten hours a day.

I think the secret to good dog ownership is really choosing a compatible breed and taking time to nurture, train, feed, and care for the dog very well.
Marc Morrone, I know, would agree and in this fascinating book makes the reader go from question to question with unflagging interest and curiosity.

Martha Stewart
March 2009

INTRODUCTION

The Dog—The Eighth Wonder of the World!

One of my favorite movies of all time is the original 1933 version of *King Kong*, and one of the scenes that always stood out for me featured the late actor Robert Armstrong, eagerly gloating over the immobilized body of King Kong on Skull Island. He announces to his shipmates that Kong's name will be up in lights in New York City as "the eighth wonder of the world!" That same scene was attempted by the equally talented Jack Black in the contemporary *King Kong* remake, but I thought that it lacked the flavor of the original—nobody can utter that phrase like Robert Armstrong can!

One thing that always stuck in my head about that "Eighth Wonder of the World" title bestowed upon the doomed Kong was the fact that Kong was a naturally occurring freak of nature. It was obvious that he should not be grouped with the recognized Seven Wonders of the World, as those were all man-made creations of ancient cultures and civilizations.

You could just as easily say that a blue whale is the eighth wonder of the world, since Kong really was no greater a behemoth than a whale. However, the true eighth wonder of the world does not swim through the ocean or live in the jungles of Skull Island. Right now, the true eighth wonder of the world is soundly sleeping in the beds of millions of people all over the world, pooping on their clean floors, chewing their furniture, and knocking over their garbage pails. The true eighth wonder of the world is the dog!

You see, the dog is indeed a "man-made" creation brought about by the pet-keeping ancestors of my viewers and listeners (and now readers) many thousands of years ago. The amazing thing about it was that these ancient pet keepers had no idea that they were even creating the dog. Unlike the Pyramids of Giza or the Hanging Gardens of Babylon, the process involved no great design. The dog happened by accident.

No one disputes the fact that the dog began as a wolf. Through domestication, the wolf was habituated to humans, and the physical characteristics and behaviors that we did not like or need were bred out of it. However, there is some controversy about how the whole process started and how and why those early pet keepers decided that the wolf was a useful and enjoyable creature rather than another animal to be used for food or clothing. I am not going to tread these waters since it really isn't too important here—what is important is how our pet keeping ancestors selectively bred the wolf traits out of the wolf without even knowing what they were doing.

For instance, suppose a wolf puppy born to a tame wolf had naturally floppy ears or a curled tail. This wolf pup would not have survived if born to wild wolf parents, as these physical traits are linked to the biochemical changes that ultimately resulted in domestication. The associated behavioral changes of decreased natural wariness, curiosity, and sociability would have compromised a wild animal's chances of survival, but one of us humans liked the pup's look and favored that animal over his siblings. As a result, that floppy-eared wolf had a chance to grow and breed and pass those traits to its offspring. Our ancestors had no idea this would happen—they just liked the animal with the floppy ears. Its equally floppy-eared puppies were just gravy!

Other random traits that popped up during this process were also maintained. Anyone who has kept wolves knows that they do not bark. They make a kind of snorting or woofing noise when startled or looking at something of interest, but it cannot be compared with the way dogs bark. Barking must have started when perhaps a tame wolf made that snorting sound in the middle of the night to alert everyone to danger when a predator approached the cave. We appreciated this talent and, when times were hard, the wolves that were best at making this alerting sound were the ones that were fed and cared for. As a result, they were able to breed when times were good and thus pass this trait to their offspring with greater and greater frequency. And 20,000 years later, I get letters every day from pet keepers whose dogs bark way too much—who would have thought?

It was only a matter of time before tame wolves were transformed into the dogs of today. When you consider the magnitude of this feat, and the chance manner in which it started, it is just astounding. Remember that all of the different dog breeds are genetically the same species with a vast amount of man-made variation between them. One need only go to the Westminster dog show in New York City and look at all of the different breeds—each one representing a particular culture or time in history—to appreciate the creation of the dog. Considering all of this, I do not believe that anyone can challenge my statement that the humble and eager-to-please dog is indeed the eighth wonder of the world.

What I find equally unbelievable is that we modern-day humans share our homes with these marvelous creatures and yet can so horribly misinterpret canine actions and behaviors. Pet keepers can become very frustrated by their dogs because they don't understand the basis for different dog behaviors. Looking at the world from the animal's point of view creates a sense of awareness of the situation. Explaining this is one of the most gratifying parts of my work. I help owners understand why their dogs are doing what they are doing and how simple it is to change their pets' behavior. My explanations give pet keepers such joy and help both the owners and the dogs in all other areas of their relationships.

Dogs are not just the eighth wonders of the world; they certainly seem to be extensions of ourselves. But in spite of that, they are still dogs—not furry humans. Dogs have done and always will do their best to please us and figure out what we want from them. However, the world has become a much busier place compared to the time when those wolves started sharing our caves thousands and thousands of years ago. All groups today needs a spokesperson to negotiate for them and to explain their needs and goals to the rest of society. This book is my opportunity to act as the spokesperson for the dog and to help you understand your own eighth wonder of the world. Understanding your dog will ensure that he complements your life rather than complicates it.

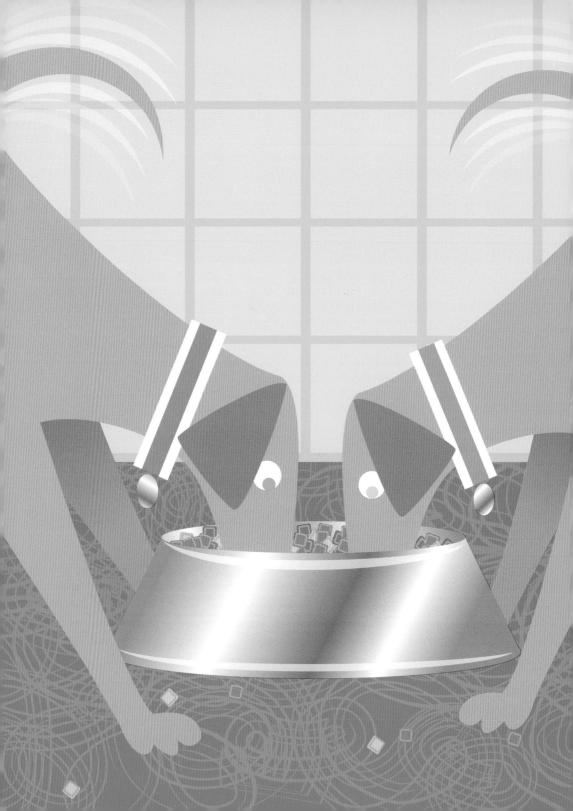

Breakfast of Champs

Twenty years ago when I started going to the Westminster dog show, I always made a point of asking everyone what they fed their dogs. And their answers seemed to go in phases. One year almost everyone would be using a certain brand of kibble, then the next year it would be canned food, and the following year they were all feeding their dogs raw diets. And you know what? Those dogs always looked fabulous no matter what they were fed.

Look at old black-and-white pictures of show dogs from the 1920s and 1930s. They looked great, and many of them were fed table scraps. Back in the 1920s, coonhounds down South were fed mainly grits, gravy, and whatever they managed to catch. And those coonhounds did a lot more work than coonhounds do today.

This shows you that dogs are very adaptable. There are no hard and fast rules for feeding your dog, and dogs can do well on many different diets.

What is better for my dog, canned food or dry food?

Although there has never been any scientific research done to prove this, in my opinion dogs do better on canned food. This is based on my personal experience feeding many, many dogs for many years. I can't say exactly why this is true, but they seem to have better coats, better skin, and generally better condition when fed canned food. Another real advantage of canned food is smaller stool volume. Of course, many dogs do fine on dry food. But if you are feeding your dog dry food, you might want to switch for a few weeks and see if you notice any difference. You know your dog best, so only you can be the judge.

How do I choose a good brand of food for my dog?

Read the label. If it sounds like something you would eat yourself or feed to your family, it's good for your dog. The first ingredient should be pure meat, not by-products, wheat middlings, or anything that sounds unfamiliar to you. The only exception to this rule would be a prescription diet from your vet. Prescription diets are formulated to help with specific health problems and may contain some odd-sounding ingredients.

Should I feed my dog a raw diet?

Many years ago when I had wolves, I had to feed them a raw-meat diet. At the time, I also had eight dogs and eight cats, and I started feeding all of them the same diet. I was amazed at the difference in the condition of their coats, skin, teeth, and gums. Even their breath smelled sweet. Dogs that are fed a raw-meat diet also have a very small stool volume.

Uncle Marc's Homemade Dog Food

CHICKEN LEGS AND THIGHS
BROWN RICE
PACKAGES OF FROZEN MIXED VEGETABLES

1. *Get a large package of chicken legs and thighs on sale at the grocery store. Boil until cooked.*
2. *Remove the chicken, but save the water that it was cooked in. Remove and discard the chicken bones.*
3. *Finely chop or grind the chicken meat and skin and put it aside.*
4. *Cook the brown rice in the water that you used to cook the chicken.*
5. *Combine equal parts of chopped cooked chicken, cooked brown rice, and thawed vegetables in a large bowl.*
6. *Divide the mixture into single-serving portions (depending on the size of your dog) and freeze.*

Microwave it before feeding. Offer your dog one portion in the morning and one in the evening. When you start feeding this diet, you may notice that he is suddenly eating more than usual because the food tastes so much better than what he was used to. In general, the dog should be allowed to eat as much as he wants at each meal, so you may need to increase the portion size at first. In most cases the dog's appetite returns to normal as he gets accustomed to the taste of homemade food, but use your own judgment. If the dog is frantically licking his empty dish for ten minutes, he probably needs more food. If he finishes, stares at you for a couple of minutes, and then walks away, he has obviously had enough, regardless of whether he thinks he should get another helping.

However, preparing a raw diet is tricky, and buying a commercial raw diet is expensive. When I stopped keeping wolves, feeding the raw diet became too expensive, so I switched my animals to canned food. But I will never forget the dramatic change in their condition when I started feeding them the raw diet. In my opinion, if you can afford it and you have the time to prepare it, raw food is always best. However, there will always be somebody who will not agree, so be prepared.

Is it a good idea to make a home-cooked diet for my dog?

Prepared commercial dog food is a relatively new thing on the dog-keeping scene. I was just looking at a 1953 issue of *All Pets* magazine, and there was not one dog-food ad in there. Dog food first came out in the 1950s but didn't become popular for a while. Before that, generations of dogs were fed on a combination of table scraps, bread, milk, and raw bones and scraps from the butcher. And they did just fine. Judging from the dogs in old movies, they stayed in pretty good condition on that type of diet. Lassie and Rin Tin Tin sure looked good to me.

In other parts of the world it is still common for people to cook for their dogs rather than to use commercial dog food. You can make a nice homemade stew for your dog from equal parts meat or chicken, vegetables, and brown rice or potatoes (see sample on page 13). This stew makes a fine diet for dogs. Cook a big pot of it on Sunday, divide it into portions, and put the portions in the freezer. An advantage is that you will never need to worry about what might be in the food that your dog is eating.

The only issue with homemade dog food is that it may lack certain vitamins and minerals. If you read the ingredients on a can of dog food, you will notice that the first eight or nine that are listed are recognizable, but the rest will be various vitamins and minerals that are added to the formula. If you decide to feed your dog a homemade diet, consult a nutritionist or veterinarian to ensure that this diet is nutritionally balanced. You will likely be advised to give your dog a daily vitamin, mineral, and calcium supplement, available at any pet-supply store.

How many times a day should I feed my dog?

Many years ago when I was a kid, most vets recommended feeding a dog three times a day until six months of age, twice a day until one year of age, and once a day thereafter. For generations, most dogs ate once a day, and they did fine.

Personally, I have found that my dogs are much more content if I feed them twice a day throughout their lives. But this is just my opinion—do what works best for your dog. Some people believe that feeding a dog two or three small meals a day can prevent bloat. But bloat is such a random event. According to vets, the only sure way to prevent it is to have the dog's stomach tacked in place. This is commonly done when a high-risk breed is having some other surgical procedure done, such as being neutered. There is no evidence to confirm that feeding frequent smaller meals will prevent bloat, but this certainly won't hurt the dog.

What are the best treats for my dog?

To me, the idea that dogs need treats all day is a little puzzling, but many people get a lot of pleasure from feeding their dogs. So if you want to give your dog treats, make sure they are good for him. Give him something as natural as possible. It's pretty ludicrous to spend a lot of time and money feeding a dog a healthy diet only to offer him highly processed dog treats full of chemicals and additives. For example, treats that resemble foods like bacon, sausage, or pepperoni are full of additives and are also very fattening. For treats, I like to give my dogs chopped pieces of apple, celery, and baby carrots. I keep them in a Tupperware container in the fridge, and when I take it out and shake it up, all of the dogs go nuts. They get so excited waiting to see what will come out of the container. They love these healthy treats just as much as fake bacon, and they are much healthier.

Do dogs appreciate the taste of fancy dog treats?

Fancy dog treats usually have more salt and fat than more nutritious treats do, and dogs do enjoy those flavors.

How fat is fat when talking about a dog? Are Whippets and other sleek dogs really underweight?

Every dog has his own unique body chemistry and metabolism, but in general, you should be able to feel your dog's ribs under his fur. Conversely, if your dog is eating normally but still looks very skinny, you should take him to the vet for blood tests and a general evaluation.

How do I help my overweight dog lose weight?

First of all, there is no such thing as an overweight dog in the sense that dogs cannot manage this feat without human assistance. If a dog is fed too much and exercised too little, this combination will have the expected effect on him. But it's not my job to judge an owner who happens to overindulge his dog. My concern is how to fix the problem. The easiest solution is to feed the dog less. But if the owner gets a lot of pleasure from feeding his dog, this isn't going to be very satisfactory for the dog or the owner.

Another approach is to feed the dog a low-calorie dog food. There are plenty on the market today. Most dogs, however, find low-fat food a lot less tasty compared with what they were used to eating. Such a dog starts turning up his nose at the new food, and the owner makes up the difference with treats. So this approach usually doesn't work either.

A better solution is to decrease the amount of calories in the dog's diet without cutting down on the volume or the taste of the food. The easiest way to do this is by adding canned pumpkin to his diet. Make sure that you use canned pumpkin—not pumpkin pie mix, which is very fattening and will completely defeat the purpose. For some reason, carnivorous animals love the taste of pumpkin. Zookeepers put pumpkins in the cages of wild animals for a treat. The animals chew on, bat around, and just love their pumpkins. Dogs are the same.

Feed your dog the same total volume of food as he is used to eating, but use canned pumpkin in place of one third to one half of his usual food. The dog will eat ravenously and feel full, the owner will be happy watching the dog eat, and the dog will lose weight!

TAP OR BOTTLED?
If you are not drinking your tap water, you should not let your dog drink it either. If you don't think it's good enough for you, it's not good enough for your pet.

Of course, this approach might not work unless you also cut out the fattening between-meal treats. If you offer fruits and vegetables instead of fatty table foods and dog treats, your dog can have as many treats as he wants. Just a warning: stay away from grapes, raisins, garlic, and onions, all of which can be harmful to dogs.

It also wouldn't hurt to give the dog more exercise. But if you have the time to give your dog more exercise, you may already be doing that. If you can't increase his exercise, cut down on the calories.

Do dogs like vegetables?

Wolves are carnivores, but dogs are omnivores. A wolf cannot survive on a diet of dog food. This change in dogs came about as part of the process of domestication. When wolves started living with humans and sharing our food, their diets included a lot of stuff they didn't eat before. These wolves got our leftovers, which may have been an old bone or some vegetables. The wolves that could digest this type of diet had an advantage—they

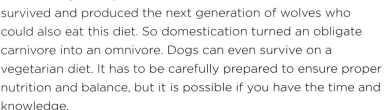

survived and produced the next generation of wolves who could also eat this diet. So domestication turned an obligate carnivore into an omnivore. Dogs can even survive on a vegetarian diet. It has to be carefully prepared to ensure proper nutrition and balance, but it is possible if you have the time and knowledge.

All of my dogs eat vegetables. They love celery, carrots, and sweet potatoes. A big sweet potato or soup carrot cut into strips is the cheapest chew toy you can find. It's great for the dog's teeth and keeps his breath smelling good.

Broccoli is an extremely nutrient-dense food high in vitamin C, among other things. Spinach is an excellent source of iron. Red peppers contain capsium, which stimulates circulation and digestion.

I've heard that some foods (such as garlic) are dangerous for a dog, while others say the same foods are fine for dogs. Who's right?

Garlic is a member of the lily family, and most vets confirm that large quantities of garlic, onions, grapes, and raisins are toxic to dogs. If you feel that any type of food is unsafe for your dog, just don't feed it to him.

Why can't dogs eat chocolate?

Chocolate contains a chemical compound called theobromine, which in large quantities can be toxic to dogs. The risk depends on both the size of the dog and the type of chocolate. Baker's chocolate and dark chocolate contain more theobromine, so they pose more risk. Milk chocolate contains very little theobromine, so you probably don't need to panic if your dog eats one Hershey's Kiss, but you may need to rush your dog to the vet if he eats a whole bag.

Why are some dogs fussy eaters?

There really is no such thing as a fussy eater. We make our dogs fussy. Feeding our dogs really is one of the great joys of pet keeping. An owner may get used to watching his small dog eat more while he is growing, but as a puppy reaches full size, his appetite tends to level off. This lessens the human's pleasure of watching his dog eat, and the usual response is for the owner to start adding things to the dog's food to encourage him to eat more. Dogs are opportunistic—in no time at all, he will learn what's going on here.

As long as your dog is pooping once or twice a day and does not spend his days pulling sleds, herding sheep, or lifting Timmy out of the well, he is probably doing fine on the amount he feels comfortable eating.

Most cats don't overeat, but dogs seem to wolf down their food until they are ready to explode. Why?

In nature, dogs eat in packs; in a pack situation, you will always get more if you wolf it down. Cats are solitary hunters, so a cat can hide under a bush and eat the mouse at his leisure. A dog has to eat fast, or else another dog will come along and take his food.

The one cat that actually does wolf down its food is the lion. Lions also are pack hunters, and they also learn that if they don't "lion down" their food, it's going to be taken away.

My old dog is losing his teeth, but he still wants to chew on bones. Will this hurt him?

As long as your vet has examined the dog's mouth, his remaining teeth are strong, and he shows no signs of gingivitis, it's fine for him to chew the things on which he has normally been chewing.

Some breeders recommend letting a dog fast for 24 hours with nothing but water. Is this good?

I personally have never heard of this, but I would imagine that the dog would be very active because he would be so hungry. The dog might not poop for 24 hours, but I don't think that this could offer any real advantage.

Can my dog's diet affect his behavior?

Diet affects the animal's overall health. If a dog doesn't feel well, is overweight, or has dry, itchy skin, he is not going to be as active or comfortable. However, aside from feeding your dog poison, which is what happened in the dog food recall of 2007, there is very little you can feed your dog that will go into his bloodstream and brain to directly affect his behavior.

What is the best material for a dog bowl? Are plastic or stainless steel bowls harmful?

Stainless steel and ceramic are the two best choices in my opinion. Many of the chemicals in plastic bowls can affect the color of a dog's nose. If a dog rubs his nose against his bowl while eating, this can cause the pigment on his nose to fade. Kibble can also cause microscopic scratches on plastic bowls. The fat on the kibble will become lodged in these scratches and can turn rancid.

The Story of Buddy

One cold winter afternoon, I was in my store, and in walked a lady with a Cairn Terrier on a leash. I thought at first that she was going to ask me to cut his nails or something. But she was crying hysterically. She walked up to me, handed me the leash, and walked out without skipping a sob.

I've always liked terriers, and this one was a beauty. He was steel gray, with a rough rugged look and a sparkle in his eye. It wasn't until I got him home that I discovered that this one was also a complete lunatic. He had the highest energy level of any dog I had ever met. He was like a canine version of Mowgli the Jungle Boy. He acted totally on instinct—and he was not house-trained. So this gave me some insight as to why the woman was crying—maybe she was forced to give the dog up, or maybe they were tears of joy because she no longer had to clean up after him!

The first thing I needed to do was try to house-train him. But this was going to be a challenge. He was not at all crate-trained, and he would bark hysterically when he was in the crate. He loved water, so squirting him with the plant mister had no effect at all. In fact, he seemed to enjoy it.

Crate-training Buddy was a unique experience. Every day I would put him in his crate in the den, and my family and I would sit in front of the TV, totally silent, not moving, until Buddy barked himself hoarse. This took about an hour. We could not move, make a sound, or make eye contact with him, or he would bark even more. We had to sit there like wax-museum dummies.

After six weeks, Buddy decided that there was no point to barking in the crate. In reality, it is best to let a dog make his own decision about something, and terriers were genetically selected to think for themselves. Once Buddy was crate-trained, I could move on to his house-training. Three years later, Buddy still has issues, but he also still has that sparkle in his eye. He is one of the smartest dogs I've ever met.

I love to tell this story to people who become impatient if their dog doesn't learn a command in five minutes or who expect their dog to be housebroken a few days after coming home.

What is the best way to house-train a puppy to relieve himself outdoors?

House-training puppies causes owners more distress than anything else. There are many different methods that have been used in different cultures over the ages. I am sure that ancient pet keepers had some method of training their wolves to go outside of the cave. It probably involved something like throwing rocks at the wolves, but it obviously worked in its own way.

In the end, all puppies eventually get the idea no matter what method you decide to use (minus the rock throwing). The method I am going to describe is the time-saving way to house-train a puppy.

The important thing to keep in mind is that you're dealing with bodily functions, and the puppy has no consciousness about them. He feels that he has to go, so he does. He can't plan ahead and try to use these bodily functions for spite.

Dogs have two hardwired instincts that will make the training process easier: they will instinctively "go" in the same place all the time, and they instinctively do not want to relieve themselves where they sleep. Take advantage of these assets that nature has bestowed on dogs, and use a training crate.

The crate is the puppy's home; it should never be used for punishment. For proper sizing, it should be as long as the puppy—large enough for him to lie down comfortably, but no bigger. If the crate is too big, the puppy will have no problem relieving himself in the crate and sleeping at the other end. Most crates for large-breed puppies come with dividers that can be removed as the puppy grows.

A puppy is going to have accidents at first, so start by putting a thick layer of shredded paper in the bottom of the crate. The paper will absorb any liquid in case your puppy does have an accident in the middle of the night, so you won't find a wet, stinky mess when you let him out at 6 a.m. After a month or so, most puppies stop having accidents in their crates. At this point, you can replace the paper with a nice dog bed or fluffy crate mat. Keep using the paper until your puppy stops having accidents, keeping in mind that some puppies take longer to adjust than others.

Put the crate near the door through which you will take the puppy outside to relieve himself. If the puppy can see the door, it becomes easier for him to start visualizing where he is supposed to eliminate. If you keep the crate upstairs, it is much harder for the puppy to get a mental concept of the process. He will have no idea how to find his way from the bedroom to the back door.

When it's time for the puppy to go out, open the crate, lift him out, put on his collar and leash, and carry him to the spot that you plan to use as a doggy bathroom. For example, in my backyard I have a 6-foot-by-8-foot space covered in "pee" gravel (get it?). Put the puppy down on your chosen spot and keep him there. He can wander to the end of the leash, but you must stay in place so that he can go no farther.

It's very likely that he won't do anything the first time you take him out to this spot. Wait ten minutes or so and then carry him back to the house and put him back in the crate. *Do not let his feet touch the floor.* Ten minutes later, repeat the process; keep doing this until the puppy pees and poops in the proper spot. If the puppy never gets the opportunity to relieve himself in the house, *he will never think it is an option.* Otherwise, when it is cold or rainy, the dog is not going to go out. He will wait and go on the clean, warm kitchen floor instead.

After the puppy pees and poops outside, you can let him run around the house, but you must supervise him all the time. If you need to answer the phone or something, pick him up, put a leash on him, or put him in his crate. If he has an accident in the house because you weren't paying attention, that is *your* fault. Just clean it up. There is no point in screaming at the puppy or putting him in the crate. Yelling might make you feel better if you had a bad day at work, but it doesn't teach the puppy anything.

The worst thing that will happen with this method is that the puppy will have an accident in his crate, which will not be a big deal since you have the shredded paper in there to absorb most of the mess. As time goes by, if the puppy has not had the opportunity to pee and poop in the house, he will voluntarily want to go to his spot outside. He will start making a connection in his mind about needing to go to the bathroom and going outside to the place where he is supposed to do this. Some puppies need more time to get the idea, but they will.

Puppies generally need to go first thing in the morning, right after they eat, and after they play, so you always need to be on guard. Particularly in the morning, some dogs need to poop twice. So if your puppy goes out but doesn't do much, he will probably need to go again.

My puppy was doing great with her house-training, but now she's started having accidents. I was also told that it was cruel to keep her in the crate.

It is typical for most new puppy owners to become a bit lax in their dog's potty training when the dog hits eight to twelve months of age, as the owners usually assume that the dog is fully trained. But as you have discovered, this is not always the case. However, the word *trained* is not really accurate to describe potty training, as we are not actually teaching the dog to do anything. Potty training is a matter of taking advantage of the two aforementioned instincts that are programmed into every dog's brain:

1. Life is better if you potty in the same place every day.
2. Do not potty where you sleep.

By keeping the dog in the training crate when you are not supervising him, you are preventing him from eliminating as long as he is in there. As soon as you take him out of the crate, you will either carry or lead him to the area in which you want him to go, be it a spot outside or on a wee-wee pad indoors. The dog will eliminate on that spot right away since he has been holding it in. Now, the key to all this, as I've mentioned previously, is to not allow the dog to ever have the opportunity to potty in the house. You don't want the dog to think that relieving himself in the house is even an option. You will achieve success only if you have the puppy under constant observation anytime that he is loose in the house. If you cannot watch him, put him in the crate or just pick him up and hold him in your arms so that he cannot eliminate on the floor.

I was told that it can be very difficult to house-train small dogs, and I am having a lot of trouble training my Toy Poodle puppy. My husband thinks this is going to be impossible. Yesterday, right after her walk, she ran into the living room, jumped on a chair, and peed.

Little dogs like yours have very small bladders and may have to urinate twice in as little time as a half hour. This is what happened when your dog urinated on the chair right after being let outside to go—she was not being watched,

she had to pee, and she just happened to be on the chair. It is all just timing and biology—there was no malice or planning on the dog's part. It is just a ten-month-old Poodle puppy who had to pee. Tell your husband to save the drama for one of life's more important issues.

Had the puppy been watched, you could have whisked her off the chair as soon as you saw her start to squat and then run her outside. Had she been in the crate, the situation never would have happened. Potty training for any dog is all about consistency and the options available to the dog, and these factors are all influenced by you. About the only aspects of house-training that you can't control are the dog's size and age.

It takes small dogs about a year and a half to get used to going only in the designated spot; big dogs take about a year. This has nothing to do with brains or breed; little dogs just have those little bladders over which they do not have too much control. Plus, your house is much bigger to a small dog than it is to a big dog. If a little dog is 30 feet away from your back door or in another room of the house when he needs to go, then he might not be able to hold it in long enough to get to the door in time.

Remember that a biological function in dogs is just that—a biological function. Dogs just do not have enough folds in their brains to figure out how to utilize a biological function to make our lives harder—they are too honest for that anyway.

> ### *LEG LIFTS*
> Male dogs usually lift their legs when they urinate. They use this as a way to communicate. Among other things, it helps dogs learn how big other dogs are, depending on how high up on the tree the urine marks happen to be.

My dog is very well house-trained at home, but he pees on everything, including me, every time I take him someplace. Why does he do this, and how can I stop it?

He does it to mark his territory. When a male dog goes into a new area, he leaves small amounts of urine on every surface to let other dogs know his name, his social security number, how much money he has in the bank, and so on. You also count as part of his territory. The only way to stop this is to keep a leash on him so you can get his attention and interrupt him before he has a chance to pee on something. You may not be able to do this if he isn't on a leash, and you probably won't be paying as close attention to what he is up to. When your attention is focused on the dog, you will know when he has the intention of peeing on something. The leash makes it a lot easier to quickly get him outside before he can lift his leg on something in the house. If he no longer gets the opportunity to do this, eventually he will stop. But it won't happen without direct intervention on your part. Dogs are creatures of habit. If they are allowed to urinate in certain places, they will keep doing it. If they don't have the chance, they will forget about it.

This is how I trained Buddy, my Cairn Terrier, to stop lifting his leg in the house. I would put him on the leash and slowly walk him through the house. Without the leash, he would have happily marked everything, but he didn't have the chance to do that. Once we got outside, his eyes were crossed because he wanted to pee so badly. Once he eliminated outside, I could safely bring him back in the house without needing to worry.

I heard that dog urine kills grass because of urine's pH level. I bought something that is supposed to change the pH level of my dog's urine, but my lawn is still full of brown spots. What am I doing wrong?

This is an old wives' tale, and it is 100 percent false. I have studied this for years. When a dog pees on your lawn, the grass in the center of the stain will be completely brown and dead, but the grass around the edges will be lush and green. Why? Because it is the ammonia, which is a form of nitrogen, in the urine that kills the grass. The same thing happens with lawn fertilizer, which contains nitrogen. If you put too much fertilizer on your grass, the nitrogen level will be too intense, and it will have the same effect.

Since the problem has nothing to do with pH level, feeding your dog a supplement to change this won't help the grass. And why feed your dog something that will change his body chemistry? The next question is: why are these products sold if they don't work? Simple—because people continue to buy them.

You may wonder how this urban myth got started. I have a suspicion. Obviously, a big dog will create a bigger brown spot on the lawn than a little dog will. A little dog relieving himself on wet grass might not even leave a mark on the lawn. Someone probably noticed this and concluded that there was something different about that dog's urine rather than realizing it was more likely as a result of the volume of urine being deposited on the grass by that dog. Beliefs like this are just anecdotal; they are not based on scientific evidence.

Urine is urine, and it always contains ammonia. If you catch your dog peeing on the grass, quickly hose it off to dilute the nitrogen concentration of the urine. Otherwise, dig up the brown spots and reseed them. Or you can do what I did: I portioned off a section of my yard with railroad ties and covered it in pea gravel for the dogs to use as their toilet. The dogs are happy, and the grass is happy.

Why does my dog urinate in front of the dog door instead of going outside?

Your dog probably has every intention of going outside, but he can't hold it long enough to get there. Sometimes dogs sense that it is cold or rainy outside, and they hesitate to go out. As a pet keeper, it is your responsibility to supervise your dog better. Remember: don't give him the opportunity to have accidents in the house. If he is hesitating at the dog door, encourage him to go through it before he has an accident.

Is it true that paper-trained puppies can't be trained to go outside?

Yes and no. A paper-trained puppy can be trained to go outside, but house-training is easier if the puppy never has opportunities to go in the house, even on paper. If he is used to going on paper indoors, it will take a while for him to get the idea that he should go outside instead. If you stay outside with him long enough, he will have no choice but to relieve himself out there. Eventually, he will start to make the connection that outside is a new OK place to relieve himself.

How do I get my puppy to use wee-wee pads?

One of the reasons why small dogs have become so popular is because people just don't have the time to house-train large dogs to go outside. It's very easy to teach a little dog to use wee-wee pads or newspaper in the house if you just keep in mind the principles we mentioned earlier when discussing training a dog to go outside:

1. Dogs like to go to the bathroom in the same place all the time—this means on the same substrate, too. Outside, a dog will always choose the same patch of grass or gravel.
2. Dogs don't like to eliminate near where they sleep.

The easiest way to train a small dog indoors is by using a puppy playpen (also called an exercise pen or "ex-pen"). Set it up in your kitchen. Cover the entire bottom of the pen with pads or newspaper so that no matter where the pup goes to the bathroom, it will be on the pads or paper. Put a small bed in the pen and use cable ties to secure it to the side of the pen; this way, the bed will always be in the same spot and the puppy can't drag it around the pen. Attach a large water bottle to the side of the pen as well. There is no point in putting a dish of water in there because the puppy will tip it over in no time, making a big mess.

Because the bed is affixed to the side of the pen, this is where the puppy will always choose to sleep. And since the entire bottom of the pen is covered with pads or paper, the puppy will always eliminate on that surface. As a result, the puppy is going to imprint on that particular substrate. After a couple of weeks of spending time in the pen, you can gradually reduce the amount of paper or pads in the pen. When the puppy is faced with the choice of relieving himself on the familiar surface (the part of the pen covered in pads or paper) or the unfamiliar surface (the bare floor), he will prefer what he is already accustomed to.

It's equally important to make sure that the puppy does not have the opportunity to go to the bathroom anywhere else in the house during this training period. When the puppy is out of the pen, your eyes must be on him all the time. If you are distracted and unable to offer constant supervision, pick him up or put him back in the pen. You must be persistent. As time goes on,

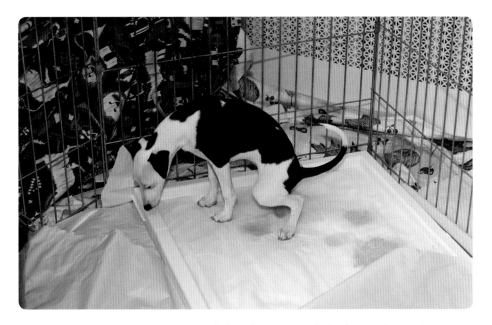

you can start putting paper or pads in other parts of the house, but only once you are sure that the puppy has identified this substrate as the place to go to the bathroom. If the puppy is regularly missing his mark when he is in the pen, it's ludicrous to expect him to eliminate in the right spot when he is not confined.

As time goes by, the puppy will come to understand proper potty behavior. You can't discipline him; he must make this distinction for himself with your help.

My dog pees whenever he gets excited. How can I stop this?

This is called submissive urination, and you can stop it by not letting the dog get excited. For example, if he normally gets excited and urinates when you come through the door, be prepared. Don't talk to him or make eye contact when you enter the house; just snap on his leash and get him outside before he goes. If he gets too excited when guests come over, be prepared. Put him in his crate while they come in. When you let him out of the crate, take him outside first, then let him come in and greet the guests. As a pet keeper, you are best equipped to anticipate your dog's reactions and prevent behavior that you don't want.

One of the First Dogs I Trained: Cindy

We didn't have cell phones when I was a kid. When my mother wanted to tell me something, she would give our dog a note and tell her to find me. (This is the way we would "text" in the '60s.) If I was down in the basement and my mother wanted a can of peas, I would give the can to our dog, Cindy, and tell her to find Mom. Cindy was so good at this.

One day when I was about twelve, my mother decided to play a trick on a friend of hers. Her friend dropped by and didn't know I was in the basement. Mom told Cindy to go downstairs and get her a can of corn. Our house was an old Victorian, and someone in the basement could hear everything being said upstairs. So I took a guess that my mother wanted to impress her friend, and I played along. However, I gave the dog a can of beans instead of corn, and she took it upstairs and gave it to my mom. My mother took the can and said to Cindy, "No, I said corn—C-O-R-N—not beans." Cindy went back to the basement, and I gave her the can of corn. My mother's friend was completely convinced that Cindy could spell.

Using treats to train a dog seems like bribery. Why should the dog do anything unless he is getting a reward?

Why should you go to work unless you are getting a paycheck? Animals don't do anything unless they see a positive result. Some dogs are so eager for our praise that this in itself is enough of a reward. But it isn't enough for many other dogs. That doesn't mean they don't love us as much—certain dogs have a stronger social drive, and others have a stronger food drive. All of the animals you see doing those magnificent tricks in films or on TV are trained using food rewards. Frank Inn, the famous animal trainer who trained Benji, always had a little plastic bag full of steak cubes on hand when Benji was filming his scenes. So if a professional dog trainer like the late, great Frank Inn needed to bribe Benji with steak cubes, why should things be any different for you and your dog?

What is clicker training?

This is a form of behavior modification that can be used to teach any animal that some type of treat is forthcoming. In other words, when we offer our dog a treat and click the clicker, he soon associates the clicking sound with the prospect of a treat. We can then modify the animal's behavior by observing him. If you want the dog to lie down on command, wait for him to lie down on his own, and then click and offer a treat. Do that repeatedly, and gradually the dog will associate the term *down* with the click and the prospect of a treat.

Clicker training is how all animals, from killer whales to birds, are trained for animal shows. It's only recently that this well-known training method has spilled over into pet animal training. All pets can be trained with clicker training, but they can be trained to do only things that are natural to their physiology.

This is a great method for teaching certain behaviors, such as coming on command, which is the most important thing for a dog to learn. It's also a great way to teach your dog to walk by your side. If you periodically click and treat while you are walking, the dog will be far more concerned with

Frisco

If you work at it, you can train dogs to understand many words. The first dog I ever trained was a Wire Fox Terrier named Frisco. He was my first dog, and I didn't realize that terriers were not the easiest dogs to train. I will never forget the first time I told him to sit and he did it. I was just amazed. My Cairn Terrier, Buddy, has the same quick reactions.

When I was ten, my parents finally allowed me to have a dog, and I got Frisco. At the tender age of ten, my parents felt I was responsible enough to take care of a dog.

Back then, we didn't use food for training; the popular training methods were shaping and flooding, and they did produce some amazing results. You can see the results of these types of animal training in the old Disney movies like *The Shaggy D.A.* or shows like *The Beverly Hillbillies*. There were so many different kinds of animals used, and they were trained to do some incredible stunts.

At that time, there also was no computer animation. Those animals and trainers actually performed all of those complicated scenes. The very best was the old version of *The Incredible Journey*. In one scene, a Bull Terrier is hurt and two bear cubs start playing around him, then the mother bear comes in to see what's going on, then the Siamese cat comes in—and all of these animals were trained to work on this scene together.

Another great scene in an old dog movie is in *Lassie Come Home*, where Lassie crawls out of a well, exhausted, and collapses on her side without shaking out her coat even though she (who actually was a he) was soaking wet. This is a very unnatural thing for a dog to do—but not for Lassie!

I had no human friends, and I spent all my time training Frisco to do all sorts of tricks and obedience commands. I entered him in a lot of obedience trials. What's interesting is that back then half the people showing dogs in obedience trials were children. Many children spent their time training dogs. You really don't see that today. Children spend more time in front of computers, and it's too bad that they find the virtual world more interesting than the natural world. The point of bringing pets into our homes is to incorporate the natural world into ours, but many still just take it for granted without any fascination about the animals that share their lives.

paying attention to you (in anticipation of getting a treat) than nosing around on the street. To see this in action, watch *The Wizard of Oz*. As Toto walked down the yellow brick road, he wasn't looking at Dorothy. He was looking to see what was in Dorothy's basket, which was full of meat cubes. Why do you think he kept trying to jump into the basket?

If you want to learn more about clicker training, there are many books, Web sites, and chat rooms devoted to clicker-training techniques for every type of animal you might want to train.

What is the best kind of collar to use to train my dog? Are you opposed to pinch collars?

In my opinion, whatever works for your dog is a good collar. A pinch collar looks fearsome, but if it has little rubber tips on the prongs, there is no way it can hurt the dog. The advantage of a pinch collar is that the dog will instantly feel pressure from the collar when he pulls; when the dog stops pulling, the collar (and the pressure) instantly releases. The dog quickly makes a connection between pressure and pulling. In contrast, the handler must pop or jerk a choke collar to get the dog's attention. The pinch collar requires no human intervention, which is why it works better. However, neither one works as well as a head halter, which is my favorite method for keeping a dog from pulling.

Have you ever used an electric collar?

I have used electric collars, and I have even put them on myself to see how hard they shock. It is not much of a shock—I would compare it with a shock from static electricity. No electric collar will make smoke come out of a dog's ears; they don't hurt the dog, but I don't particularly like them because I don't care for negative-reinforcement training methods.

There are situations, though, in which negative reinforcement is warranted. For instance, if a dog will not stop chasing livestock, drastic measures are needed to prevent him from being shot by farmers. If your dog is barking so much that your neighbors are complaining and you are faced with either getting rid of your dog or being evicted by your landlord, a no-bark electric collar is a good thing. The electric collar is a tool, and it is not to be abused. Use it only when circumstances warrant it.

What is the hardest command to teach a dog to obey?

Dogs learn all behaviors the same way. Teaching a dog to come when called when off lead is the hardest because people tend to go about it the wrong way. They order the dog to come instead of teaching the dog that coming when called is the best thing in the world. However, if the dog thinks that something good will happen every time he comes to his owner, it's easy.

How do I teach my dog to come when called?

Ordering your dog to come on command will not work. You need to teach the dog that when he hears the word *come*, it's a signal that something good awaits him if he returns to you. You can start by putting the dog on a short leash, telling him to come, and giving him a treat when he does.

When I was a kid training my first dog, Frisco the Wire Fox Terrier, we were told to use a long leash and reel the dog in if he refused to come. I improved on this by attaching a fishing line to his collar. I started with the short leash, then I used the long leash, and then I used the fishing line. Frisco thought there was some unseen force compelling him to come back to me. It worked, but of course he was a little terrier; it might not work for a German Shepherd. It is just easier to teach the dog to come back to you for a treat. If you don't want to keep your pockets full of dog treats, get a bait bag. This is what the handlers use at dog shows. You can clip it to your belt and always have treats handy.

How do I prevent a noisy dog from barking?

Dogs do whatever works for them, so if making noise gets results, they will make noise. Look at it from your dog's point of view. The dog sees the mailman coming toward your house, walking directly and purposefully, getting closer and closer and finally right into the dog's territory, so the dog barks more and more. Then the mailman turns around and leaves, but he comes back six days out of seven.

A dog can become obsessive about this, and owners can make the problem worse by inadvertently encouraging it. If you stop what you are doing and start paying attention to the dog by telling him not to bark, he is going to misinterpret your actions and words. The dog is going to think that you are equally worried about the mailman intruding into your territory, thus your effort to quiet the dog completely backfires.

If your dog constantly barks at people on the street, put up a fence to block his view. Some books recommend distracting the dog when he barks with a stream of water from a water pistol. This works, but I prefer to use 1-quart plant misters. They hold a lot of water, and I just leave them all over the house. The dogs only need to see me pick up a mister, and they know to be quiet.

Distractions also work, but this method takes more time, and many owners don't have the time to train their dogs this way. All of my dogs are clicker trained, so all I need to do is make a clicker sound, and they immediately stop whatever they are doing because they know that this sound means a treat is forthcoming.

It's always easiest to use the fastest, most convenient method. "No-bark" collars also work for a quick fix. They distract the dog with one of various things, usually either a spritz of citronella, a vibration, or a shock. Some behaviorists criticize the use of these collars, but if you are getting complaints from your neighbors or facing a lawsuit because of your dog's barking, you don't have a lot of alternatives. Your dog would rather keep living in your house and wear the collar during the times when he is out in the yard.

My dog is addicted to getting into the trash. No matter where I hide it, he finds it. Any suggestions?

Yes, it's called a baby lock. Put your trash in a cupboard and put a baby lock on the cupboard door. Or take your trash out before you go to work, which is what we do. If a dog can get into the trash, why shouldn't he? It brings him so much pleasure. Dogs love garbage, and they can smell it anywhere.

I was told to turn my back and ignore my dog to stop him from jumping on me. This isn't helping. What else can I try?

A lot of this depends on the dog. Turning your back is a good method, but you may have to do this 150 times before he gets the idea. Some dogs will happily jump against your back. There are many other ways of stopping a dog from jumping up. Years ago, the preferred method was to bend your knee so the dog got a knee in the chest. That worked, but some dogs also got injured. However, they did learn not to jump.

I think the easiest way is to put a leash on the dog. Step on the leash before he jumps, tell him to sit, and praise him. It all boils down to the reward factor. If the dog continues to be rewarded for jumping, even if the reward is unintentional, he will keep doing it. Dogs jump because they are rewarded with attention, which can be anything from touch to talking to eye contact.

Of course, some breeds, like Irish Wolfhounds, are almost required to jump on people when posing for pictures. This is a slow-moving dog, and it's probably more of an inconvenience for him, but it's always fun to see a picture of an Irish Wolfhound on his hind legs, putting his paws on someone's shoulders.

Do dogs ever fake being sick to get out of doing something?

That kind of behavior would involve conscious planning for future events, which dogs can't do. Dogs live in the moment. Relatively speaking, there is nothing we would ask a dog to do that could encourage him to plan that way even if he were able. If you ask your dog to take a bath and he doesn't want to, he will simply run away and hide. If your dog doesn't want to get in the car and go to the vet, he will run away and hide. Dogs give immediate responses to events taking place at that moment. They have no ability to deliberately plan to avoid a future event. If that were the case, we would be the ones wearing the collars and leashes.

BUTT SNIFFING
Dogs sniff to learn about one another. If a dog wants to do this but isn't really sure of the other dog's intentions, it is much safer to stay away from the end with the teeth. There is much less chance of being bitten if he smells the other end.

Do dogs have a sense of their size?

Every dog has a strong sense of self. When they judge size, dogs are not thinking of themselves as much as they are thinking whether things around them are bigger or smaller. The way a dog reacts to this depends on his individual personality and experience. A little dog that was raised with big dogs will probably feel more tolerant toward them. But if a little dog has had bad experiences with big dogs, he may be afraid or aggressive.

Do dogs always growl first before biting?

No, and I can tell you that from personal experience. I have been bitten by many dogs that never warned me with a growl.

My scariest dog-bite experience happened with one of my own dogs. For years I wanted a Scottish Deerhound. I was enthralled with English literature, and I envisioned myself with a cap, a tweed jacket, and a Deerhound. Finally, I got a beautiful show-quality Deerhound from a breeder in Florida. That dog was the apple of my eye; I just adored her. One day, my family came to visit, including my three-year-old niece. She had been raised with dogs and loved them. Out of the corner of my eye, I watched this dog jump on the couch in the den as my niece walked toward her. The dog never growled or acted aggressively, but her eyes flashed yellow. I sensed trouble and snatched my little niece just as the dog grazed her arm. It wasn't a bad bite, but it could have been.

The only time I was really savaged by a dog also came with no warning. A woman brought her Vizsla to the shop and asked me to cut his nails. I sat on the floor, cradling the dog on my lap, and cut one nail. The dog went berserk. I tried to get him in a headlock, but he bit me pretty badly. I got patched up, and I was fine a week later.

Oddly, my worst dog bite in terms of complications was really tiny; only one tooth punctured my skin, but it was the wrong tooth. The wound became badly infected, and I ended up on intravenous antibiotics.

How do I stop my dog from pulling on the leash?

When I was a kid, teaching a dog to heel was very time consuming. We used choke chains, which are now called training collars. It was a very involved process, riddled with negative reinforcement. The dog would forge ahead, you would yank the leash and tell him no, and eventually he would stop pulling. But because this process was so tedious, a lot of people just didn't bother. Thus, there were many dogs who were either pulling their owners' arms out of the sockets or choking themselves.

Now people avoid training their dogs to heel and use harnesses instead of collars. When wearing a harness, a dog can pull all he wants. This works fine for a little dog, but big dogs are another story.

There is a device that will teach your dog not to pull right from the get-go. Visualize the way a horse is led around. A horse never wears a collar and leash; a horse wears a head halter with the leash under his chin. If he pulls ahead, his head turns around. He might be able to walk backward and drag you, but not forward. The same system works for dogs.

The biggest problem with the head halter is that it doesn't fit as close as a horse's harness does. Be sure it is fitted correctly on your dog. Halters come in different sizes, but every dog is slightly different. It is best to try the halter on your dog at the pet-supply store rather than trying to estimate the right size. While you are there, also buy a tandem coupler so you can attach your dog's leash to both his collar and the halter. This will ensure that he cannot get loose if he slips his head out of the halter.

The second step, after fitting the halter correctly, is to train your dog properly so he never thinks about slipping his head out of the halter. Never begin this training outside. If the dog is distracted and starts a rodeo act and manages to slip out of the halter, he will know this is possible, and he will always try to do it. Put the halter on him in the house, leading him around with your hand for a few minutes. Don't attach the leash until he adjusts to this sensation. Next, practice with the leash in the house for a few days.

Don't start training outside as long as the dog is balking and fighting the halter. Once he accepts the idea that the halter does not come off, he will accept the idea that his pulling days are over. The only problem you might run into is that the halter looks like a muzzle, and people may start thinking that your dog bites.

What motivates my dog to chase a bird or squirrel?

The dog descended from the wolf, a predatory animal, and this instinct still exists in every dog, from a big Saint Bernard to a little Chihuahua. The predatory instinct is triggered when a dog sees a small object moving away from him. The predatory instinct will motivate a dog to chase a squirrel or a ball or a mechanical rabbit around a track, as all of these things trigger a response to chase.

When they do catch a squirrel, many dogs don't know what to do with it. They don't even think about that when they are chasing it.

LOOSE DOGS
If your dog is running around and you need to get him back quickly, sit or lie down on the ground and call him. Nine out of ten times he will come to you, not because he is worried if you are OK but because he will think you might be eating something, and he will want to investigate.

My dog hates fences. How do I stop him from scaling, jumping over, or digging under my fence?

Some dogs are such great escape artists because we don't put them in securely fenced areas when they are puppies. A puppy behind a 2-foot-high fence will quickly learn how to climb or jump over it. Once he acquires that ability, he will immediately try to do the same with a 4- or 5-foot-high fence. It's the same thing with puppies who learn how to squeeze under fences. They will continue trying to do that with every fence they encounter.

The key is to prevent the dog from ever learning how to escape. Puppies should be kept in secure areas so they never have the option of a successful escape. If the dog has already mastered the art of escape, training him to stay in a fenced area is more complicated. If he digs under the fence, you must run mesh wire along the ground where it meets the bottom of the fence. It has to extend far enough away from the fence to discourage him from trying to dig under the mesh wire. To keep him from going over the fence, you need to put mesh wire along the top, angled inward. When the dog gets to the top of the fence, he will hit the wire. This method is commonly used in zoos to keep large wild animals inside their compounds. If it works for a tiger, it will work for your dog.

How can I tell if my dog has separation anxiety?

It's pretty hard to tell if your dog has separation anxiety because you are not there to see the dog after you leave, but you need to understand what constitutes what we call "separation anxiety." A dog that is bored while his owners are at work will chew up curtains, rugs, chair legs—basically the whole house. The dog wants to chew, and there is no one to stop him. A destructive chewing problem can be resolved simply by keeping the dog in a large crate with many safe toys while you are at work.

A dog that doesn't like being in a crate sometimes paces back and forth, bunching up his bedding in one corner in the process. The dog then becomes anxious because he has to lie on the bare crate floor. To prevent this, line the crate with 6 to 8 inches of shredded newspaper, and hide treats and toys in the paper. If he paces, the paper will pack down rather than bunching up in one area. And he will spend so much time rooting through the paper to find the goodies you've hidden that he won't have time to be anxious.

Calling these behaviors "separation anxiety" is anthropomorphic. In reality, we are attributing human emotions to the dog. However, if your veterinarian has determined that your dog has a psychological problem, there are prescription medications that can be used to control anxiety caused by a chemical imbalance. These work very well, but they must be used under veterinary supervision.

Why does my dog attack the vacuum cleaner?

Dogs rarely see the vacuum cleaner, so it can be frightening for a dog when you take it out. You use the vacuum all over the house, and the dog chases it, barks at it, and tries to bite it. Finally, you turn it off and put it away. The dog thinks that he either has chased it off or managed to kill it. If you turn the vacuum cleaner on and leave it near the dog for six or seven hours, he will eventually realize that it's nothing to worry about. Instead of attacking it, he will no longer give it a second thought. And his life will be much easier.

None of my dogs bark at the vacuum cleaner. In fact, I even use it to vacuum their coats so they don't shed all over the house. They just lie there, and we vacuum them. Any dog can learn to tolerate things that look strange or make strange noises. Just look at any street dog. These dogs don't blink an eye at trucks, buses, or construction sites because they are used to seeing and hearing them.

My Pointer is always biting my hands. He started doing this as a puppy, and I thought he would grow out of it, but it is getting worse.

Anyone who has seen puppies play knows that they bite one another's ears and tails. This is part of puppy behavior. When you take a puppy away from his littermates, he will then try to play with you, his new littermate, in the same

way. If he has a chance to bite your feet, clothes, or hands playfully, it may seem cute at first. As he grows up, it's not so cute.

Never let a puppy's teeth touch your skin; then he can never think of you as a plaything. I'm not saying that the puppy shouldn't play; that's part of being a puppy. But you must redirect a puppy's mouthing behavior—from body parts to toys—from day one. All members of the family must be strict about following this rule. If one person lets the puppy play roughly, the puppy will think it's OK. If you let your puppy bite your hand one time and stop him nine times, he will decide that he can try biting you ten more times. This is called the "slot-machine" effect. When you go to Atlantic City and put a quarter in the slot machine, you don't get a bundle of money for each pull of the lever. But the idea that you might get a bundle of money makes you try again and again. The same idea applies to dogs who try to play roughly with people. If you are inconsistent in your corrections, he won't get the right idea. Instead, he will keep repeating the behavior, knowing that eventually you'll let him get away with it.

Redirect your puppy's play to toys, and consistently refuse to let him play roughly with you. If you let down your guard and let the dog take your hand in his mouth just one time, you'll be back to square one.

How do I keep my dog from chewing up the furniture?

Dogs have no concept of money. A dog will never understand that some things have value and others don't. If you have a dog toy, a shoe, and a pocketbook on the floor, the dog will make no distinction among them. Whichever item gives him pleasure at that moment is the one he will pick up and chew.

It is our responsibility as pet keepers to be sure that the dog has no access to shoes, pocketbooks, or furniture. The only way to do this without using a training crate is to live in a house made of cement, with cement furniture, no shoes, and no pocketbooks. The dog would have no other option but to chew on his toys.

Since completely blocking your dog's access to forbidden items isn't possible, you must use a training crate when your dog is young and in his exploratory phase. When your dog is in the crate, he has no opportunity to chew on objects other than what you give him in the crate. When he's not in the crate, it's up to you to prevent him from chewing on things he should not be chewing. It's your responsibility to make sure that his only choice is to chew on his toys.

How long will this training take? Every dog is different. Some dogs mature more quickly than others do. By six months, some puppies no longer need the training crate, while others, such as Boxers, can act like puppies until they are up to three years old.

All dogs eventually learn what is OK to chew. Every culture has dogs and its own ways of training dogs, and they all seem to learn the rules. My method is designed for a busy person who doesn't have time to monitor his dog all day. I developed these little tricks based on my own experience, which I am happy to pass on to you. Other methods work, but mine is less time consuming and involves the least amount of confrontation with the dog. Unfortunately, there are a lot of humans who thrive on confrontation and think nothing of confronting an animal as simple and basic as a dog.

My dog goes crazy in the car. How can I make him stop whining, pacing, and panting for the entire trip?

Your dog is unhappy in the car, so you need to make him comfortable. The easiest way is to sit in the car with him every day. Don't go anywhere—just sit there. Read a magazine, turn off your cell phone, and just enjoy the peace and quiet. If you are calm, your calmness will radiate to the dog. Eventually, he will decide that being in the car is fine. Just keep sitting in the car with him day after day until he is calm; then start going for short drives. Needless to say, your dog should always be placed in a secure crate during car trips. In the Care chapter, you will read about how I learned this lesson the hard way when driving with my dog Barney.

Uncle Marc

Many people think I'm a veterinarian and call me Dr. Marc instead of Uncle Marc, which is my preferred title. This started when my little nephew Nicholas was three years old and used to help me in the store. When he wanted something, he would call "Uncle Marc, Uncle Marc," and pretty soon everybody called me Uncle Marc.

However, there is no way in the world I could have been a vet, and I have the greatest respect for vets. For people to think I'm a vet is the ultimate honor. Veterinarians have it very tough. Getting into vet school is difficult, and a veterinary degree is one of the most expensive educational programs you can pursue. Earning a veterinary degree also requires many years of study and incredible self-discipline, which I don't have. Our doctors need to know about only one species—humans—but veterinarians need to know everything about all types of animals, each of which needs different drugs, different forms of anesthesia, and different surgical procedures.

People also assume that I must have some degrees in order to know what I know. I barely graduated high school, and other than that, all I have is a library card and a Social Security card. So I need to rely on veterinarians to take care of my pets, just as all of my listeners, viewers, and readers do.

Your dog can't tell you which vet is best; you must make this choice. In my opinion, a veterinarian who is a kind and approachable person can be a better choice. The vet who is a nice person will have compassion and will admit when he or she doesn't know the answer. This kind of vet will be more willing to help you find someone who can solve your animal's problem. And for some reason, many people are afraid to communicate with their vets. If someone's vet says something that the person doesn't understand, the person walks out of the office scratching his head rather than saying, "Look, could you please explain this?" This is what I say all the time.

If the vet is very busy or distracted, find out when you can call and discuss the problem in greater detail. Veterinary treatment is often a process of trial and error. If a urine test reveals that your pet has a bacterial infection that can be treated with five different antibiotics, the vet will start with drug A. If that doesn't work, he will move on to drugs B, C, and D—and E, if needed. It is your responsibility to tell the vet which drug is working rather than being angry because drug A didn't work and now you are faced with paying for drug B.

If your funds are limited, be honest about this with your vet. When you take your pet to the vet, rather than saying, "Do whatever it takes to make him better," tell the vet how much you have budgeted for veterinary expenses. That way there won't be any surprises for you or the vet. Lack of communication causes problems in both human-pet and human-human relationships. For the sake of your pet, it is important to have a professional and friendly relationship with your vet. This isn't impossible. All of the vets who take care of my pets are also very good friends of mine.

How often does my dog need shots?

This is a hot-button subject these days. As a general rule, most vets no longer feel that annual vaccinations are necessary—except for rabies, which is required for all dogs every one to three years, depending on the type of vaccine that is given and individual state laws. When you take your dog for his regular checkup, you can ask your vet to draw blood and check his titer levels to ensure that he has enough antibodies circulating in his blood to protect him from distemper, parvo, etc. When the blood titer levels are low, then he needs another vaccination.

I heard that vaccinations are dangerous for dogs. Is this true?

Vaccinations themselves are not bad for dogs, but too many vaccinations can be bad for some dogs. Other than the rabies vaccine, which every dog must have within a time frame determined by state law, it is safer to confirm that vaccinations are needed rather than administering them as a routine preventative measure. Many vets now offer in-office titer testing. However, a test confirming a high titer is not a legally acceptable substitute for vaccinations that are required by state law.

What should I do if my dog is stung by a bee?

It depends on where the dog is stung. First, make sure that the stinger is removed. After that, almost anything you apply will be licked off by the dog immediately, so there is not much you can do besides rinsing off the area and applying cold compresses. Although most mammals have far more tolerance for bee venom than humans do, a few dogs will have severe reactions to bee stings. If this is the case with your dog, you should immediately take him to the vet because he could experience anaphylactic shock. Of course, if you are worried in any way, go to the vet. This will give you far more peace of mind than anything you are going to read in a book.

What is the safest way to remove a tick from my dog?

There is much difference of opinion about this. Some pet-supply stores sell what's called a "tick key," a little piece of metal with a teardrop-shaped hole that can be placed over the tick to pull it right out. A pair of tweezers will do the same thing. Some people recommend covering the tick with Vaseline to smother it or holding a hot match up to it.

The important thing is to pull it out completely. I prefer not to pull a tick out with my fingers, but I have done it when I don't have anything else handy. I can't look at a tick on a dog without wanting to get it out. Some animals, such as giraffes, have birds that sit on their backs and pull out the ticks. I'm sure that these birds aren't using Vaseline or tick keys.

What is the best way to get rid of fleas? Why do they keep coming back?

Before the topical flea-control products like Frontline and Advantage came along, the only way to get rid of fleas was to wash your dog in poison (aka flea shampoo) every week. Flea shampoo killed only the fleas on the dog at that time, so this treatment had to be repeated every time a new bunch of fleas hopped on your dog. The nice thing about the newer topical products is that they are secreted from the dog's pores for a month. When new fleas jump on the dog, they immediately die and fall off. These products are reapplied monthly.

> **REMOVING QUILLS**
> Porcupine quills have extremely strong barbs at the end, and pulling them out the wrong way will cause the dog immense harm. You should always let your veterinarian do it.

It was said that feeding a dog brewer's yeast would keep fleas away, but I have never found that to work. Fleas keep coming back because the world is full of fleas. Winters are not as cold as they used to be, so many more fleas survive the winter.

To the best of my knowledge, there is no natural remedy that will kill fleas. There is an old wives' tale that a fox will get rid of its fleas by grabbing a leaf in its mouth and jumping into a pond. As the fox swims back and forth, holding the leaf, the fleas rush up to the fox's head to avoid drowning. As the fox lowers its head into the water, all of the fleas rush onto the leaf as if it were a little lifeboat. Now the fox is free of fleas, and the fleas float away on their own version of Noah's ark. This is a lovely story, but I have yet to see a flea that is version of Noah's ark. This is a lovely story, but I have yet to see a flea that is bothered by water in any shape or form. And I have yet to see a fox that was not covered by fleas, ticks, and mites in the summer.

How can I stop my dog from getting carsick?

Just as some people get seasick, some dogs are prone to car sickness. In some cases, motion sickness drugs can work, but it is better to desensitize the dog to car travel because the underlying problem is anxiety. We use the same process as described in the School chapter. Start by sitting in the car with the dog, with the car turned off. Bring something to read, and stay there as long as you can. Do this for a few days, or however many days it takes for the dog to be OK with it, and then move on to the next step. Get into the car with your dog, turn the car on, and just sit in the driveway, letting the car idle for as long as you can sit there. Repeat this for several days. Don't move on to the next step until your dog is OK with this. When he is calm, the next step is to drive around the block. The key is to stop each lesson before the dog becomes anxious. Little by little, increase the amount of time he spends in the car. Once he realizes that nothing bad is going to happen, he won't become anxious and therefore sick.

It also helps to make sure that the dog is secure in the car. My dogs all travel in crates, and they are blissfully unperturbed for the entire trip.

What is the easiest way to give a dog a pill?

Most people who have dogs know how to poke a pill down a dog's throat. This is the easiest way, but some people don't feel comfortable doing that. Years ago, when I was a kid, we would wrap the pill in a little piece of bread or cheese, but some dogs are too clever and will eat the food but spit out the pill. Nowadays, "pill pockets" are the easiest way. These are meat-flavored moist chews that you wrap around the pill. The texture holds the pill inside, and even cats can't get them out. They work great for dogs and cats.

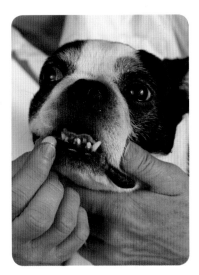

I heard that microchips cause cancer. Is this true?

A microchip is a pretty innocuous thing. It turns on for only a second when a scanner is placed over it, and for many dogs this may never happen even once in their lives. Dogs can develop many kinds of cancers and tumors in many different places. Many dogs also have microchips. This is merely a coincidence. There is no scientific evidence that microchips cause cancer.

The pet store sells so many vitamins and supplements. Do my dogs need all of them?

As a general rule, most commercial dog foods have more than enough vitamins and minerals. If your dog were pulling sleds or running races or herding sheep, then he might need more than what is provided in dog food. However, for your average dog that sleeps all day while you are at work and goes for a half-hour walk each morning and evening, the vitamins and minerals in dog food are enough.

If you are making your own dog food, it is important to add supplements to it. Your vet might also recommend added vitamins and minerals if your dog is older or compromised in one way or another. Antioxidants like vitamins C and E can be very helpful.

One thing that most dog foods don't seem to have enough of is fatty acids, which are very good for dogs' coats. One of the best sources is flaxseed oil, one teaspoon for every ten pounds of body weight. I give this to my dogs every day.

> ### DOUBLE TEETH
> Some small-breed puppies may not lose all of their puppy teeth when they are supposed to. Then the adult teeth start growing in, and this causes crowding. Chewing can help loosen retained puppy teeth, but if your puppy still has puppy teeth by six months of age, your vet can remove them when the puppy is neutered/spayed.

What is a hot spot?

A hot spot is just a local area of skin dermatitis. Some dogs get these all over their bodies in response to allergens in their environments. If only one small area of a dog's skin is exposed to an irritant, such as flea bite, the dermatitis will be localized.

You can get remedies, such as drying agents for hot spots, at pet-supply stores, but you should see your vet rather than rely on advice from a store employee. The condition of your dog's skin is an indication of his overall health.

Can a dog be allergic to grass?

Technically, dogs are not allergic to grass even though they can have allergic reactions after coming into contact with grass. Allergic reactions could result from pollen, fertilizer, or something else on the grass. Your vet can test to find out exactly what external factor is causing the problem.

Do I really have to brush my dog's teeth?

If you ignore your dog's teeth, they will go away. Dogs today can live for fifteen to seventeen years, sometimes longer. This means that teeth designed to perform their function for ten or eleven years now need to last for seventeen years. In other words, many dogs outlive their teeth. To prevent your dog's teeth from meeting an early demise, you need to clean them. Feeding kibble will not make up for good dental care at home—it would be the same as trying to keep your teeth clean by eating a bowl of dry cereal.

Can we get dogs sick? Can dogs get us sick?

There are very few zoonotic diseases that dogs and humans can get from each other. Ferrets can catch a human cold virus, but dogs cannot. Ringworm, which is a fungus, not a worm, is probably the most common thing you can get from a dog. Rabies is the most dangerous, but it is a pretty rare disease these days, and dogs are vaccinated against it.

A dog's teeth are covered in bacteria and can transmit germs to us. I've already mentioned that I was bitten by a dog once and ended up on intravenous antibiotics because the wound became so infected. A dog's mouth is not a clean place, and you can pick up a lot of bacteria by kissing your dog on the mouth, which is probably not a good idea.

Should I get health insurance for my puppy? How about for an older dog?

I have health insurance for all my pets. It's not as good as health insurance for humans, but it helps out by reimbursing you for a portion of covered veterinary expenses. For example, if your dog needs to have an operation, it's good to know that you'll get some of your money back. Policies vary, so check the fine print before choosing one. Most of them do not cover preexisting conditions, so it's better to insure your dog as a pup rather than waiting until he is older.

At what age is it safe to spay or neuter a puppy?

This depends on your vet. I have had dogs that were neutered at six weeks old and dogs that were neutered at ten years old. It has never made much difference in my experience. Some vets feel it is healthier to wait until the dog is fully grown, while other vets will tell you that a young puppy recovers from the surgery more easily. Every dog is different, so it's best to ask your vet.

What is bloat?

An affected dog's stomach twists around on itself, closing off the ends. This has the dual effect of causing gas to build up and cutting off the blood supply to the stomach. This leads to shock and eventual death if not treated immediately. Large, deep-chested breeds are most prone to bloat, but it can happen to dogs of all sizes. It is a life-threatening condition, requiring emergency surgical intervention.

There are a lot of recommendations about how to prevent a dog from developing bloat, such as avoiding feeding the dog certain foods, dividing his daily food portion into several small meals, discouraging him from exercising shortly before or after a meal, encouraging him to eat his food calmly and slowly, and not allowing him to gulp water. These precautions are thought to reduce the possibility of the dog's swallowing a large volume of air. One recommendation that has been discounted by newer research is the value of feeding your dog from raised dishes. Many dogs eat from dishes on the floor without developing bloat, and recent studies suggest that raising a dog's food and water bowls actually contributes to the risk of his developing bloat.

There is a new procedure that is becoming more common in breeds that are predisposed to bloat. When a puppy of a bloat-prone breed is being spayed or neutered, the vet will surgically tack the pup's stomach in place to prevent it from twisting. None of these are foolproof methods, though, and you can only try the best you can to prevent bloat. Otherwise, preventing bloat is really the luck of the draw.

Are there any advantages to a raised feeder?

Although raised feeders may not be recommended for all dogs, they may be good for dogs with reflux or vomiting problems. For you, the benefit of a raised feeder is that it will keep your back from hurting when you pick up the dog dish.

Why does my dog have tear stains, and how can I get rid of them?

The jury is still out on exactly what causes tear stains. Some dogs produce excess tears, which cause reddish-brown stains that look particularly ugly on white dogs. There are some topical remedies sold in pet-supply stores that are supposed to remove tear stains, but they typically don't work very well.

One thing that really helps minimize tear staining is keeping the fur on the dog's face clipped short. Long hair acts like a wick, spreading the stains to the rest of the dog's face. Once you clip this hair, though, you must monitor it because it can grow back with a bristly texture and start irritating the dog's eyes as it gets longer.

Another thing that works to control tear staining is an antibiotic called tylan or tylosin. This is mainly used to treat upper respiratory infections in birds. It is not a prescription medication that must be purchased from a vet; it is an over-the-counter bird antibiotic, but giving small doses to dogs can stop tear staining. Vets can't really explain why it works, but it does.

There is some controversy about treating cosmetic problems with antibiotics, but no dog feels good with big wet patches on his muzzle all the time. Chronic tear staining can lead to skin irritation or infection if left untreated. There are obviously some bacterial issues involved with the process that respond to this antibiotic, but the staining will come back when you stop giving the tylan.

This is a temporary measure, and you must find the underlying cause to stop tear stains. There can be quite a few reasons for excessive tear production, such as allergies, ear infections, dental problems, or hair falling into the dog's eyes. Keeping the dog's eyes clean and dry will help, but you should consult your vet for a permanent solution to the problem.

How do I deskunk my dog?

There are so many recommendations for how to remedy a skunk problem. Tomato juice is the traditional method, but I have never had much luck with that. I personally use a mixture of one part hydrogen peroxide, one part baking soda, and one part dishwashing soap. Mix it into a paste, rub it through the dog's fur, and let it sit for a while before rinsing it off. I've found this to work

the best. Nature's Miracle also makes a skunk-odor removal product that does a good job.

Can dogs get Alzheimer's disease?

I wouldn't call it Alzheimer's disease. As dogs get older, they are going to slow down mentally and physically, but scientific research has yet to confirm that this form of dementia is the same as Alzheimer's in humans.

Is it safe to give your dog natural remedies from the health-food store?

That depends on what the remedy is for. Supplements such as different types of fatty acids are fine. However, it's not a good idea to give a supplement to treat a medical condition. I never play doctor with my pets. If I don't know what's wrong, I grit my teeth, pay the money, and get the right answer from the vet. I am certainly not going to rely on a clerk in a health-food store to diagnose my pet's health problem and prescribe a human remedy to treat it.

The Canine Mystique

Although we know quite a bit about dogs, some things remain a mystery. Some of these are funny, such as why some dogs watch television and others don't, which I will address later in this chapter. These dog behaviors and abilities have yet to be explained by modern science. Why can some dogs smell cancer? How can some dogs predict an epileptic fit? How can some dogs find their way home over vast distances?

Most dog behavior is clear-cut because it is based on instinct, although as humans, we often try to attribute human motives to animals' puzzling ways. But there are some canine instincts, talents, and abilities that just have us totally shaking our heads.

My dog wants to play ball all day long. He never stops. How can I make him leave me alone for a while?

If you don't want to play ball with your dog, just don't. He knows if he drops the ball in front of you over and over again, eventually you will give in and throw it.

I have a dog—Garfield, the big brown mutt—that does the same thing. He will stand there with the ball in his mouth, staring at me. I have to sit in my chair with my eyes riveted on my book because if I make eye contact, he will think we are going to play. Every now and then, he paws or nudges me. I tell him to back off, and he will sit down with the ball in his mouth. If I get up, right away he's there with the ball. This might be the time I'm going to play ball with him, and he's determined not to miss that opportunity. He is actually doing this to me right now as I write this!

My dog always seems to know when it's time for dinner or a walk. How does he do this?

Well, animals do have a good sense of time. Anyone who has seen the movie *Lassie Come Home* is aware of this. At a quarter to four every afternoon, Lassie knew it was time to go to school and escort young Roddy McDowell home, even when she was thousands of miles away in Scotland.

Animals can certainly tell time, but they do it a bit differently than humans do. Most of our pets learn about our daily routines from watching our behavior. For instance, when your dog sees you get out of your chair and pick up the leash, it's walk time. Dogs can also figure things out by watching our eyes. If we look toward the kitchen, we are thinking about making dinner.

Why does my dog insist on burying his toys in the couch cushions? This has become very embarrassing when guests come over.

This happens in my house all the time. All wild canines dig holes and bury things they want to save for later—this is a latent ancestral instinct in dogs. In cartoons and movies, dogs are shown turning around and digging backward to bury things, but they really use their noses to push the dirt forward.

If your dog is outside and decides to hide something valuable, he will dig a hole in the yard. If he happens to be in the house, he will hide his treasure someplace, like under the couch cushions. He can't bury it in the floor or carpet, but he can poke and paw at the couch cushions until it is hidden to his satisfaction. The dog may not even be aware that he is doing this because the behavior is directed by instinct.

Why does my dog eat his poop?

To this day, no veterinarian has been able to give me a definite answer to explain this puzzling behavior. Everyone seems to have a different opinion, but I don't think that the dogs are listening to what the vets have to say. Some people recommend putting hot sauce on the poop to make it taste bad, but it's poop—how good can it taste to begin with? And wouldn't it just be easier to pick up the poop so that the dog isn't able to eat it?

For small dogs, adding meat tenderizer to the dog's food works about half the time, as this helps maximize digestion so that the dog won't be attracted by rice, corn, or peanuts still whole or visible in the stool. However, it won't work for all small dogs, and large dogs seem to have such a high food drive that it has no effect on them. There is only one thing I have found that really works. If the dog doesn't get a chance to taste any poop for several months, he will lose the desire to eat it. It's like ex-smokers who smell cigarette smoke a year after quitting and wonder how they ever enjoyed smoking in the first place. This method will work only if the dog has absolutely no opportunities to eat poop for many months. You really have to watch the dog carefully and keep your yard cleaned up.

Why do dogs eat cat poop?

Compared with dog food, cat food is much higher in protein. To dogs, it's like an elixir. On top of that, the cat's litter box is usually right in the middle of the floor, sitting there like a buffet for the dog. If you were at home and could watch the dog all day, you could say "No" every time the dog went near the litter box, and eventually the dog would stop. But most dog owners don't have the time to constantly watch and correct their dogs, and it won't work if you do it only some of the time.

You need to make the litter box inaccessible to the dog. The cat's not going to do it. At my house, I solved the problem by putting the litter box in a closet with a sliding door and leaving the door open only 6 inches. The cat could easily fit into this gap, but it was too small for the dog. This worked fine until I got a little dog who could also get into the closet. I solved that problem by putting the litter box up on a small table. Anything will work as long as the box is inaccessible to your dog(s) and accessible to the cat.

Why do dogs eat grass?

There are lots of myths about this; the most common one is that dogs eat grass to make themselves throw up when they don't feel well. That sounds plausible, but dogs don't think that way. They are more straightforward and incapable of reasoning that eating grass will alleviate stomach trouble. They eat grass because they like the way it tastes, especially if it isn't always available, which is often the case. They have no grass in the winter, and it dries up in the summer, so when they find some luscious green grass in the spring, they eat it. We can only guess the reasons why dogs eat a lot of strange things. They also eat shoes, drywall, paper, tables, and chairs. They eat all of these things, but it never has the effect of settling the dog's stomach.

Unfortunately, many species, like humans and dogs, cannot digest grass. Their digestive system is not designed for that. Humans discovered that they can digest the grass seeds, which led to the cultivation of wheat. For dogs, it is a simple in-out procedure. Since the dog cannot digest the grass, it eventually has to come back out the same way it went in.

Why do dogs roll in stinky stuff?

I have read that dogs do this to disguise their scent and that this habit was inherited from wolves. That sounds like a great explanation, but unfortunately dogs don't think that way. As we've mentioned, dogs live in the moment and are not capable of the cognitive reasoning behind such a behavior. Dogs roll in stinky stuff simply because they like it. As they live in the moment, this response is just a hardwired instinct. Their reaction to something that smells good to them (although we may not agree!) is no different from your reaction to the smell of a basil leaf or a nice perfume. It isn't a preconceived idea, but when you smell something good, it suddenly occupies your mind for that moment in time.

Some dogs love wearing clothes so much. Why?

Dogs work for two things—food and attention. Circus dogs and TV dogs love their jobs so much because they love the attention. It's the same for show dogs. When you watch a dog show, you can see how much those dogs enjoy what they are doing.

Likewise, when you put clothes on a dog and he gets a lot of attention, he quickly learns that wearing clothes gets him what he wants. If wearing a T-shirt or a bandana brings attention, the dog will look forward to dressing up.

My dogs can tell when we are going on TV just by watching my actions that day. They get very excited because they know that when they are on TV, they get a lot of attention. When you have as many animals as I do, they don't get as much individual attention as they would like. When we are on TV, they each get more attention, so they are all for it.

How do you toughen up a scaredy-cat dog?

You can't "toughen up" a dog that is timid or scared. You need to let the dog encounter scary situations, and make sure that these situations always end on a positive note. Eventually the dog will realize that there is no reason to be scared. It has nothing to do with being tough; rather, it's the dog's perception of a situation. Once the dog changes his perception, he will choose not to be scared any longer.

You can help a dog change his perception of a situation by exposing him to the situation enough times. For instance, if your dog is afraid of traffic and loud cars, take him to a bus stop and sit there all day. Read some magazines as your dog takes in the sights and sounds. Eventually he will stop associating traffic noise with danger. Behaviorists call this "flooding." Another method is to use positive reinforcement. Every time a car goes by, reward the dog with a treat. The dog learns that when something "bad" happens—the car going by—something good will also happen—getting a treat.

You can only help the dog along in this process. The actual change in perception must come from the dog.

Why do some dogs howl?

Howling is one of the few parts of the wolf that remains in the dog. This is one of the most primitive responses, driven by a deep basic instinct. Wolves will howl in response to the sound of other wolves howling. Very few dogs ever have the chance to hear wolves howling, but other sounds can trigger this response, such as the siren from a fire engine, organ music, high-pitched singing, and other dogs howling. In dogs, this response is not as instinct driven, and the response is more easily triggered by a variety of auditory stimuli. It is a combination of learning and instinct. Dogs often learn how to howl by imitating one another.

My dog is afraid to walk on grass. How can I cure this?

In the dog's mind, walking on grass is unpleasant, and nothing you do is going to change his mind. If you try to reason with him or cajole him, it will only draw more attention to the problem. He is not going to take your word for it that the grass is safe.

Treat his dislike of grass as a routine matter. Put the leash on your dog and walk him near the grass, toss some treats into the grass, and ignore him. Use the "Hansel and Gretel" approach—just keep crumbling treats and leaving a trail in the grass. Pretty soon, he will decide for himself that the grass is fine.

My dog was very friendly when he was a puppy, but now he has started acting shy. What's going on?

Young puppies take everything for granted. They follow along, accept things, and don't make many decisions for themselves just yet. That is why socialization is so important, especially for dogs that are kept singly and spend most of their time in the house alone. As a dog gets a little older, he will start making decisions for himself. If not properly socialized, he will start making random judgments and coming to negative conclusions about the world, and he will get quirky.

When I was growing up, puppies and dogs were free to wander the neighborhood all day. They had plenty of socialization and experienced many things this way. Of course, today that would be a death sentence for a dog. He would be hit by a car within minutes. You need to make up for this by taking your puppy to a puppy kindergarten class or hiring a dog walker to come and take him out several times a day. This kind of socialization will help him make positive judgments about the world and have a stable and confident disposition.

Why do dogs chew their feet?

This behavior is common to any animal in an unnatural situation. Birds chew their feathers and horses crib (arch their necks and swallow air while gripping parts of their stalls with their teeth). Wolves are so busy trying to survive that they don't have time to become bored or look for ways to amuse themselves. Dogs, on the other hand, have a lot of free time in which to be bored and obsess about things. Their feet are right there in front of their noses and are more convenient than the furniture legs for chewing.

If your dog is chewing his feet out of boredom, you can use the same preventative measures used to stop this behavior in zoo animals. Zookeepers use enrichment devices, such as puzzle-type toys in which food is hidden, all over the animals' enclosures. Similar toys are made for dogs. Before you go to work, hide food puzzles and treats around your house. Your dog will be so interested in looking for these that he will forget about chewing his feet. However, this bad habit varies from dog to dog, and sometimes it is not this easy to stop.

In rare cases, it could be caused by a food, seasonal, or flea allergy or from a yeast or bacterial skin infection, so start with a veterinary exam.

Why do many dogs hate having their feet touched?

Dogs' feet and nails are very sensitive, so it is natural for dogs to expect handling to feel uncomfortable. A dog will reflexively pull away when you reach out for one of his feet. More than anything, dogs fear the unknown.

This is at the basis of the problem, but you can't judge an animal for being an animal.

Many dogs can be desensitized if you have the time to work with them. Squeeze and manipulate your dog's toes every day, starting out slowly and working up to a little more each day. Wild animals in zoos are trained to have their feet handled for examination and nail clipping, so you can certainly train a dog to have his feet handled.

Why does my dog bark at the TV?

I don't know the answer to this one. I get letters all the time from people who write that their dogs watch me on TV and bark at the animals. However, none of my dogs seems the least bit interested in watching me on TV. My brother's Springer Spaniel, though, is an avid TV dog, to the point where he runs around to check the back of the TV when something races by on the screen.

I have consulted many ophthalmologists about why some dogs watch intently and others ignore the TV. They have theories about the number of rods and cones in the individual dog, but I really don't think they have the answer either.

It is true that some dogs can become obsessed with watching TV. If a dog sees an animal or person on TV he doesn't like, he will start barking, and eventually the object of his dislike always goes away. This reinforces the idea that the dog chased the person or animal away, especially since the scenes on TV change so quickly. This can lead to a lot of barking. Be thankful if your dog doesn't like to watch TV—life is easier that way.

How can my dog tell there's going to be a storm?

Dogs can feel the changes in the atmosphere before a storm. We also have this ability, but dogs' senses are sharper than ours, making it easier for them to detect changes in barometric pressure. This also explains why some dogs become apprehensive when a storm is coming. Dogs fear the unknown, and in this case they can sense that something is changing but are not quite sure what it is.

Dogs react to storms in different ways. Some dogs will bark. My dog Buddy runs around, barking in defiance of thunderstorms. He always succeeds in chasing the thunder away. Many dogs will ignore a storm and sleep through it, while others will be frightened.

Dogs can be desensitized to thunderstorms so they no longer fear them, but trying to rationalize your dog's fear by talking to him or sitting on the floor and comforting him won't help. Animals make their own decisions about what to fear. The best approach is to ignore the dog and not make a big deal of his fear. You can also get a recording of a thunderstorm and play it at home until the dog starts ignoring it.

Why does the tail wag when a dog's excited?

Wolves, jackals, and foxes all wag their tails. The tail is a flag used to signal thoughts and intentions to other animals. A tail is highly visible and can be seen clearly from a distance. If a dog is too far away to get a good look at another dog's eyes or ears, he can still see what the dog's tail is doing. Of course, a wagging tail isn't always a friendly tail. You need to look at the whole package to get an idea of what a dog is thinking.

How can dogs tell how we're feeling? All predatory animals must be perceptive in order to find prey. If a wolf is watching a herd of caribou, the wolf is not going to pick the strong, healthy caribou as prey. The wolf will try to find a caribou that is not feeling well or that is weak in some way by looking for one that is limping or holding its head down. Signs like this help the wolf determine what the prey is thinking, its state of well-being, and so on. Dogs use the same tricks to read us. They watch us all the time because they know that we are connected to the good things in their lives. They don't want to take a chance on missing something good, so they pay attention to us and try to anticipate what we are going to do next. There might be something in it for them!

Why does a neutered male dog still hump?

Dogs do this as a sign of dominance. If a dog mounts another dog, he is showing his dominance over that dog. He wants to exert his dominance without a confrontation, and humping is easier than using his teeth.

Why do some female dogs hump?

Again, as a sign of dominance. If a dog allows him- or herself to be humped, it shows that the other dog is considered dominant. It's nonconfrontational, and most dogs prefer to settle these matters without growling and snapping.

I have three dogs. How can I tell which one is dominant?

Certain dogs are dominant in certain areas. In my house, if all of the dogs are lying on the floor, Buddy can mount every single one of them—and he is much smaller than some of them. However, when they are eating, Garfield is the one who can nudge every other dog out of the food bowl. So Garfield is the dominant dog for food, and Buddy is a dominant dog just for the sake of being a dominant dog. When you have a group of dogs, their relationships are not quite as cut-and-dried as we would like to believe.

The little dogs I bring on TV with me are Piper, Murphy, and Dixie. Piper is a very low-key Pug, Murphy is a hyper Chihuahua mix, and Dixie is a very laid-back Dachshund. Of the three dogs, Murphy is definitely the boss, except when feeding time comes along and Piper takes charge. Politics and dominance are ever-changing in dog society, just as in human society.

Knowing When It's Time to Give Up

My Pug, Piper, is the gentlest, sweetest dog. She does absolutely nothing wrong. But she refuses to go up and down stairs. Now, in a perfect world, I'm sure I could teach Piper to go up and down stairs. If I had all the time in the world, I would put bits of cheese on each step. And Piper, like all Pugs, is completely food oriented, so I'm sure she could learn to go up and down steps that way. But I don't have the time to devote to this kind of behavior modification. It's just easier to pick up the dog and carry her up and down the stairs. Sometimes you just have to wave the white flag and put up with some of your dog's quirks. If it's OK for the pet keeper to admit defeat, it's OK for you too.

My dog never wants to play with other dogs in the dog park. Is there something wrong with him?

No, he just doesn't want to play with other dogs. Maybe, just like some children, he would rather be sitting in the corner, listening to his iPod or texting his friends. You can't force a dog to like other dogs. You have to observe your dog in order to figure out exactly what he doesn't like. It could be that the other dogs are bigger, more rambunctious, or more aggressive than your dog, and he doesn't feel safe in that situation. It might be time to find another dog park.

The solution might be as simple as going to the dog park at a time when there are only one or two other dogs there. This will give your dog a chance to get used to the other dogs in gradual steps. It's no different from a child who doesn't want to be thrown into a daycare program with twenty other screaming kids. If introduced to a few kids at a time, he may feel more comfortable when he's eventually in a group of twenty other children.

The Biggest Myth About Dogs

I was a lonely child growing up. At that time, a nerd wasn't classified as a nerd, he was just the kid that got picked last for sports teams. And there was no "zero bully tolerance" at schools. Getting beaten up was a daily occurrence for me. So I lost myself in the natural world because that's where I felt comfortable and accepted. I read a lot of books, including a lot of fiction. Many of these books were so well written that I thought they were factual. My favorite author was Albert Payson Terhune, a Collie breeder in New Jersey in the 1920s. I actually have an autographed copy of one of his books. Along with breeding beautiful Collies, he wrote great stories about them. He saw dogs as cognitive beings, capable of rationalizing situations and drawing logical conclusions. I inevitably grew up thinking that this was true, a belief that was reinforced by watching Lassie pull Timmy out of wells every Sunday night.

I was not the only person who grew up thinking that dogs had much more brainpower than they actually do. And this myth still persists today. People really believe that their dogs are rational, sentient beings. I'm not trying to downplay canine intelligence. I love and respect dogs; however, I've come to the conclusion that dogs basically act on instinct and truly live in the moment. Dogs react to situations hoping that something good—praise or food—will result. Dogs don't plan their days around trying to make us happy, as much as we would like to think that they do. I have no problem with anyone who chooses to believe that myth, but it does cause problems when people attribute every aspect of a dog's behavior to conscious reason. In this case, when a dog does something we really dislike, we don't simply dismiss it as the behavior of an animal acting on instinct. Instead, we conclude that the dog is spiteful, jealous, or some other miserable emotion that is unique to human beings. I think that the only emotion that dogs share with us is love.

Many dogs are surrendered to shelters because owners decide that behavior like peeing on the floor or knocking over the garbage is done intentionally. *If we simply let go of this misconception, far fewer dogs would be mistreated or abandoned by people wanting to teach their dogs a lesson.*

Can a dog's behavior ever be spiteful?

As I've said, dogs don't have the cognitive ability to plan ahead and do things this way. A good analogy is the squirrel that buries nuts in August. This squirrel was probably born in June and has no idea when winter is coming. Burying nuts is not a conscious plan to prepare for winter; it is just an instinct. In the same way, the squirrel stumbles across these nuts in December.

Dogs live in the moment. If you leave the garbage can sitting out and your dog is bored, he will knock it over. Owners sometimes assume that their dogs feel guilty about this type of behavior because when they come home from work, the dogs are slinking around. Rather than acting guilty, your dog is probably acting fearful because you customarily yell at the dog when you come home. The dog has no idea that your yelling is connected to the garbage can incident. But if your dog expects yelling when you walk in the door, you need to take a look at your role as a pet keeper.

When I brought my dog home after a week at the boarding kennel, he immediately ran into the bedroom and peed on my pillow. Did he do this because he was mad about being left in the kennel?

He definitely didn't do it because he was mad. Most likely, he ran into the bedroom because he was happy to be home—so happy that he peed. Some dogs will mark their territory, and the bed is the most precious place for most dogs. From the dog's point of view, that is the center of his territory.

If there were any conscious effort on the dog's part, it was probably a desire to mark his territory as an announcement that "I'm home, and this place is mine!" Of course, it also could have been just an accident.

Do dogs have hair or fur?

Technically, dogs are animals, so they have fur. But there are all kinds of dog fur. Some dogs have very fine, long fur that does resemble human hair.

Certain breeds are described as hypoallergenic, and people do ask me about dogs with hairlike coats, thinking that this coat type will be OK for their allergies. The first thing I ask such a person is if he has been to an allergist about his problem. A common answer is something like, "No, but my friend Gracie has a Bichon and I never get sick when I visit Gracie. But I have an allergic reaction whenever I visit so-and-so who has a Golden Retriever." The person could be allergic to any number of things in that home, but he won't know unless he is tested.

Some breeders use the "hypoallergenic" claim to help sell puppies, and some prospective owners use it as an excuse just because they happen to want a Bichon.

A few years ago, I got a letter from a famous allergist explaining that allergies are caused by skin dander, not fur (or hair). He wanted me to read the

letter on my show. I told him he was welcome to come on the show and address the issue, but he never did.

So what does *hypoallergenic* really mean when talking about dogs?

It means nothing. There is absolutely no scientific evidence to support such an idea. Some breeds are smaller, with finer fur, and they shed less. That is often misinterpreted to mean that they are hypoallergenic.

Unfortunately, most of the people who claim to be allergic to dogs have never been tested to confirm this. Their evidence is always anecdotal rather than scientific. Maybe someone visits a house with a German Shepherd and sneezes, but he visits someone with a Poodle and feels fine. Based on that, he decides that some breeds must be hypoallergenic. This kind of story gets repeated and people believe it, but there is no scientific evidence to prove that allergy sufferers can tolerate some breeds as opposed to others. You cannot make these determinations from anecdotal evidence; you need to consult an allergist before concluding that you are allergic to dogs.

If people really are allergic to dogs, they can do one of two things: get allergy shots or get a dog. Both of these methods have the potential to alter the immune response that triggers the allergy through repeated exposure to the allergen. The allergic person will do a lot of coughing and sneezing first before getting over his allergy. However, because of individual variations in immune function and allergy sensitivity, neither method is 100 percent effective. Interestingly, a few years ago research proved that children who grow up with pets are far less likely to suffer from pet-related allergies.

Do dogs dream?

At this point, we don't have the technology to discover what dogs dream about; they will keep that secret for a while. But many species, including dogs, do have REM sleep. You can tell that your dog is in REM sleep if you see his closed eyes moving and legs twitching.

Can tug-of-war make a dog aggressive?

The jury is out on this one. I would say that it depends on the dog and who is doing the tugging. Some experts say that an owner should always make sure that he, not the dog, is the winner at tug-of-war to prevent the dog from getting any ideas of dominance. But I don't think this is true. To the dog, this is a game. The dog knows it's a game, not a test of wills. If a dog wins a round of tug-of-war, the first thing he does is give you the toy so you can start another round.

Do dogs age seven years to a human's one?

This was the belief for many years, but this calculation was determined decades ago. It's not so simple. The dog's first year is equivalent to twenty human years. Today, both dogs and humans are living a lot longer. The average life span for a person is now around eighty, and many dogs live to around fifteen rather than ten or eleven. So that averages out to more like five dog years to every human year.

How long could my pet dog last in the wild?

No dog can survive indefinitely in the wild. There are feral dogs, but they always live near areas of human habitation where they can eat garbage or steal things (like chickens) for food. The only dog that can live in the wild is the Dingo because it reverted from a domesticated to a feral state thousands of years ago. You cannot turn any dog loose in the woods and expect him to exist like a wolf, fox, or coyote.

To the best of my knowledge, there are no wild dogs occupying an ecological niche that was left when wolves were exterminated. At one time, wolves, coyotes, and foxes occupied all of North America. Wolves today are running around Yellowstone Park, but they no longer exist in many areas where they were once prevalent, such as the British Isles, Ireland, and Germany's Black Forest. Although the wolves have been gone for hundreds of years, these regions have not been repopulated by packs of dogs. Throughout history, dogs have been abandoned repeatedly in all of the places where wolves were exterminated, yet this has not resulted in large packs of feral dogs. Dogs have formed packs and tried to survive like wolves, but in all cases they have failed miserably without human assistance to survive. This doesn't necessarily mean that humans went out and fed them, but they did provide access to human garbage dumps or domesticated livestock. A domestic dog gone feral would not be able to survive for generations solely on natural foods the way wolves do.

In the wild, dogs always succumb to starvation or parasites, or they are shot for bothering livestock. A dog might catch a rabbit or deer now and then, but not enough to sustain him over time. Dogs cannot breed and reproduce in a wild situation. So how long would your dog last in the wild? Not long at all unless some human was helping him.

I have a rescue dog, and he is very shy. Do you think he was abused before I got him?

Many people like to think that their dogs were abused and that's why they are shy. If that's what it takes to make someone adopt an animal, I'm all for it. But most dogs are shy because they did not have enough interaction with the outside world during their formative period. This lack of socialization is actually a form of abuse. Many people get a puppy and don't want to bother training him or taking care of him. They leave him tied up in the backyard and, as a result, he grows up completely unsocialized. This dog will view new situations with aggression or fear. No one was physically harming the dog, but his critical socialization period came and went, and he was never given the chance to learn about life. Now it becomes your responsibility, as a pet keeper, to expose him to new things in a nonthreatening way so that he becomes comfortable with the world around him. When unknown factors become known, his fear and worry will disappear over time.

Garfield, My Rescue Dog

Garfield is my biggest dog and also the most gentle. He was born in a burrow under a car at Kennedy Airport and hauled out with a catch pole when he was eight weeks old. He was extremely shy and frightened. His mother was a small, shorthaired, black-and-white dog. I don't know what his father was, but Garfield grew up to resemble a giant shaggy Belgian Tervuren. He is a behemoth. Despite his early puppyhood and his size, he is the gentlest, most patient, most easygoing dog I've ever owned. If he perceives any kind of threat, he will just hide. He wouldn't dream of hurting any human or any animal.

So when people speculate about a puppy's upbringing and temperament, you have to remember that a lot results from genetics and environment. If you raise the dog to be good, he will be good.

Why are Poodles' coats trimmed in such peculiar ways?

A popular explanation is that the various Poodle haircuts were designed to keep the dog's joints and shoulders warm in the water. The fur was left in these areas, and the rest of the coat was trimmed close so that it didn't soak up so much water and weigh the dog down. Poodles are water dogs, so that's a good story, but I can't imagine a fisherman bothering to give his dog a haircut like that, especially when other water dogs don't get haircuts. Water spaniels have the same coat type and do the same work that Poodles do, and no one has shaved them in similar patterns.

Poodle coats are cut that way because people in Poodle clubs determined that this was how they wanted the dogs to look. Anyone showing a Poodle must present the dog in one of the grooming patterns specified in the breed standard. Parts of the Poodle pattern were originally utilitarian, such as keeping the dense, curly coat clipped short for cleanliness. Tying up the topknot with a bright ribbon had two advantages: it was easier for the dog to see and easier for the hunter to spot his dog in the underbrush. But most aspects of modern Poodle trims are purely decorative in origin. Shaving some parts of the dog to the skin will not help keep him warm, regardless of the particular details of the clip.

Is it true that hounds will always run away if they get the chance?

You have to understand that the hound is not "running away," as that would imply that the dog is trying to get away from something. Hounds were bred to follow a trail to its end as the hunter ran along behind him. And a hound won't come back until he has caught the rabbit, the criminal, the bear, or whatever he has been chasing. Even a little hound like a Beagle will follow a scent no matter what is in the way, be it cars, backyards, or playgrounds. Even if you yell at the dog to come back, his instinct will tell him to keep on the trail.

The Beagle likely will come home the next day, after he is finished following the trail. The problem is that he will probably be hit by a car or picked up by animal control before he can do that. Huskies have a similar instinct. They run ahead as the musher encourages the dogs to keep going. If you start chasing and yelling at your "runaway" Husky, he is not going to stop, because he thinks that he's doing exactly what he should be doing.

The best way to deal with a dog with a tendency to run is to have a secure fence.

Is it true that pit bulls bite harder than any other breed?

Pit bulls are big strong dogs, and they do have the ability to bite harder than many other dogs do. But every dog can bite hard, and any dog bite will hurt. Pit bulls have this reputation because they were bred for gameness centuries ago when they were used for fighting bulls. If the dog grabbed onto the bull's nose and never let go, he was considered to be very game and would be used for breeding to pass this trait on to the next generation.

The real problem is that many pit bulls are owned by bad people. Many breeds have been in this unfortunate situation, among them Akitas, Dobermans, and Rottweilers. Dog preferences among bad people have varied over the years. But in general, bad people own bad dogs (this is referring to the individual dogs, not the breeds). And right now, their preference is the pit bull. This is ironic because the pit bull was bred to never bite people. They were bred to fight bulls and other dogs but to be very gentle with people.

When irresponsible people encourage their pit bulls to be nasty and bite, we hear about it in the news. Such owners usually don't bother to neuter their dogs and often don't care if their dogs run loose. Many pit bull attacks could be prevented with a lock on the gate that costs less than $10.

Don't blame the dogs—or the breeds—for these situations. If pit bulls were outlawed, bad people would then start keeping Golden Retrievers or some other breed.

Is it true that a dog will always throw up if he eats something poisonous?

Not necessarily. Thousands of wolves, coyotes, and foxes have been poisoned over the years by animal management programs. It depends on the poison. Many first aid manuals tell you to induce vomiting if you suspect that your dog has been poisoned, but I prefer not to take chances in an emergency like this. If your dog has ingested something caustic, vomiting can make the problem worse. And owners are often not sure exactly what the dog ingested. Whenever I suspect that something is wrong with one of my pets, I put him in the car and immediately rush to the vet.

Do dogs get worms from eating candy?

If that were the case, we would all have worms from eating candy. Dogs get worms in one of two ways: either they ingest worm eggs in the feces of other dogs, or

they acquire the worms from their mothers. When we deworm a dog, we kill all of the worms and eggs in its digestive tract. However, females can have worm cysts in their mammary glands. These can be reactivated during lactation and thus infect the puppies as they nurse. These worms will not be killed by giving deworming medication to the mother, so the puppies also need to be dewormed when they are old enough to tolerate the medication.

Does a ticking clock or a hot-water bottle help a puppy settle down and sleep?

It depends on why the puppy isn't sleeping. Many young puppies will cry all night after they go to new homes because they miss their littermates. A ticking clock may help distract such a puppy, at least a little bit. In my opinion, nothing helps as much as leaving a light on for the first few nights. If the puppy wakes up in a strange kitchen, in a crate, and in the dark, he is going to be more apprehensive because he can't see what's going on.

Regardless, you have to let the puppy cry even if it breaks your heart; otherwise, he will learn that crying is a good way to get attention. The only time this isn't advisable is when there is a chance your neighbors might complain. In that case, get a sleeping bag and sleep on the floor next to the puppy's crate. If he doesn't feel alone, he won't cry and instead will become accustomed to sleeping alone in his crate.

My Pet Wolf

DOGS

Canine Anatomy

ALL ABOUT BREEDS

What I Learned from My Pet Wolves

I learned a lot about dogs from the keeping of wolves. I always wanted a wolf, and I started by getting a wolf hybrid, but hybrids cannot even be compared to true wolves. It took 20,000 years to turn a wolf into a dog. Domestication took the wolf out of the dog, and crossing a dog and a wolf combined the worst of both species. Wolves are shy; they disappear when humans are around. Hybrids have the dog's protective nature and the wolf's strength, which can be a very dangerous combination, and a wolf-dog hybrid is a true abomination in my opinion.

Over the years, I have had three wolves. Do not get a wolf. Wolves may have made good pets for people living in caves 20,000 years ago, but not in this day and age.

Wolves can be trained only by using strictly positive reinforcement. Unlike dogs, wolves learn by observation. A dog might jump at the door to let you know he wants to

go out, but a wolf will try to turn the door handle. A dog will paw at his bowl if he wants water, but a wolf will try to turn on the faucet.

Living with wolves also taught me a lot about dog behavior. Additionally, I learned just how different dogs are from wolves—it made me appreciate dogs all the more. For instance, why do dogs bark? Wolves don't bark; rather, they make a warning sound, sort of a "chuff," by snorting air through their cheeks. For early man, this was probably very useful. The wolf stood at the mouth of the cave, and the "chuff chuff" sound woke everyone to warn them of the approaching bear. They then killed the bear, and everyone had dinner (not to mention that they avoided being attacked by a bear!). The following winter, when everyone was starving and there was only enough food for one wolf, which one would they have fed? They would have rewarded the wolf that saved everyone from the bear. Then, when that wolf had puppies, those puppies would have inherited the primitive bark. Unfortunately, being humans, we don't know when to quit, and now we have dogs that bark all the time.

What's the strangest breed of dog you've ever met?

The oddest breeds I've ever met were Dingoes and New Guinea Singing Dogs (pictured). Both of these breeds are extremely primitive, and looking at them is

like going back in time. They were among the first breeds domesticated by humans from wolves.

The most impressive dog I've ever seen was a Mastiff at the Westminster dog show that weighed well over 200 pounds. He was in perfect physical condition. Petting him was like petting a lion, which I have also done.

If you asked me to name my favorite breed, I couldn't do it. I have had so many breeds, and when I go to a dog show I fall in love with one breed until I see the next one. Reading *Big Red* as a child made me want an Irish Setter, a dog I've yet to have. *Rin Tin Tin* made me want a German Shepherd, and the Lassie stories made me want a Collie. These stories were so good, and these breeds were described in amazing detail. The writers had incredible knowledge of their breeds.

The Fox and the Hound by Daniel Mannix is also a wonderful book. He went into so much detail about different hound breeds—foxhounds, Bloodhounds, and Redbone Coonhounds. It is an amazing book if you want to learn about hounds.

I'm not suggesting that anyone should buy a dog impulsively based on something they've read or seen. These classic books and movies portray just a few wonderful breeds. There are hundreds. This makes it harder to narrow it down, but there is a perfect breed for everyone. Some of these breeds are well known, while others are not. So it pays to do your research before making a choice.

However, dogs come into and go out of my life with no planning on my part. It's rare that I do get to choose a dog, but if the time comes when I can choose one, I will get a Lurcher. The Lurcher is not a recognized purebred. These dogs originated as gypsy dogs of Europe, a combination of terrier and Greyhound. They were poachers' dogs. They would sneak onto private land in the dead of night and steal whatever game they could. And there is a certain rough and rugged look about this breed that I happen to like. I can picture my grandfather having a dog like this on his farm before he emigrated from Italy to New York in 1921.

Are designer dogs really improvements over their parent breeds?

You have to look at all facets of this situation. Every breed of dog recognized today as a purebred was at one time a "designer dog." Most dog breeds resulted from someone's deciding to cross different breeds in an attempt to combine the desirable traits of each into one new breed, and there is nothing

wrong with crossbreeding to create a new breed.

On the other hand, people will decide to cross dogs for no reason at all. Let's say you're a commercial breeder with a less-than-perfect-quality Shih Tzu who doesn't conform to the breed standard. Because you know that this Shih Tzu is not good quality, you decide to cross it to a Yorkshire Terrier, also of poor quality. Now, instead of having poor-quality Shih Tzu or Yorkies, you have "Shih Poos," and you don't need to worry about the fact that the puppies

Martha Stewart

I have worked very closely with Martha Stewart and her pets for over a decade. She called me out of the blue one day and asked me to be on her show, and I've been working on her TV show in various incarnations ever since.

Martha Stewart is a pet lover extraordinaire. Unlike many rich and powerful people, she personally cares for all of her pets. This has always impressed me.

In addition to her chinchillas, cats, and canaries, Martha had three Chows when I first met her. The male was Paw Paw, and the females were Zuzu and Empress Wu. Paw Paw was one of the most amazing dogs I've ever met. He was much like Martha. When he was at Westminster, he acted just like a show dog; with other dogs, he was just another dog; and when he was with kids, he was like a big teddy bear. He adapted himself to any situation with good grace and never did anything unwillingly. His tail was always wagging, and his eyes were always bright. In his mind, the glass was always half full, not half empty. He was a real canine optimist.

On Martha's TV show, he would stroll onto the stage in front of hundreds of screaming fans and just sit in his basket, calmly taking in the whole situation. If I was doing a show with fifty other animals bouncing all over the place, I could put him in a basket right in the middle, and he would calmly enjoy the attention.

Unfortunately, dogs don't live forever, and now Martha has French Bulldogs named Francesca and Sharkey who appear on her show all the time. One day, one of Martha's employees was driving them from upstate New York to the Hamptons, and they stopped by my store to pick up some pet supplies. The two Frenchies came in, sat in the corner, and watched everything going on. Another customer came in and began admiring the pair of beautiful French Bulldogs. She commented that they looked just like Martha Stewart's dogs and asked me their names. I introduced her to Francesca and Sharkey, and she replied, "What a coincidence. They have the same names as Martha Stewart's dogs. I see them on her TV show all the time." Suddenly, she realized that they were Martha's dogs, and she threw herself on the floor and started hugging them. Then she pulled out her camera and asked me to take a picture of her posing with Martha Stewart's dogs. Francesca and Sharkey were happy to pose with this true fan, but they unfortunately could not give her any autographs.

don't conform to the respective breed standards of the Shih Tzu and Yorkie. And you can probably get more money for them than you could get for poor-quality Shih Tzu or Yorkies.

There is nothing wrong with this as long as the puppy buyers realize that they are buying cute little shaggy mixed-breed puppies rather than puppies that were selectively bred.

Relatively speaking, what's wrong with a Shih Tzu? And what's wrong with a Yorkie? They both have a nice look, and they make nice pets. There is no reason to cross them together except to possibly benefit the person doing it. This person doesn't have to worry about registering his litters with a recognized registry or making sure that the puppies conform to recognized breed standards. I'm not trying to make anyone feel bad about their designer dogs. They all make nice pets, but they should not be misrepresented.

Are all purebred dogs inbred?

Dog breeding doesn't work the same as human genetics, in which constant outcrossing is the normal procedure. Dog breeds were created by mating dogs that possess the same desirable traits, and traits run in families. Every purebred was originally created this way. Traits like better hunting or herding skills were important for obvious reasons. Eventually, through repeatedly breeding related individuals, every dog in that family possessed a particular set of traits. These gene pools were also small because the first breeds were kept isolated to prevent random breeding and the loss of important traits. In that way, inbreeding is a useful tool. It stabilizes the traits that we want.

People sometimes assume that inbreeding means crossing together two dogs with obvious genetic defects. In actuality, inbreeding means just the opposite—crossing together two dogs with obvious virtues. There is a much better chance of recreating this trait in the next generation if the parents are related in some way. Of course, closer breeding also raises the odds that unwanted genes will pair up. This is always a possibility, but the risks should not be overstated. Many dogs do not have genetic defects, and some defects can be detected through genetic screening. This testing was not available years ago, and some dogs that carried defects were inadvertently bred, producing defective puppies. Many of these defects would not show up until later in life. As a puppy, the dog would look fine, and the problems wouldn't start until two or three years later. Fortunately, today there are many tests available, and serious breeders test their stock before they breed. Problems arise when inbreeding is done without giving equal consideration to appearance, health, and temperament. If a dog is perfect in all of these respects, it can be inbred almost indefinitely without problems.

But dogs are living creatures; they are not manufactured. And anything can happen to a living creature. You can get a dog from the best breeder and something bad can still happen—that's part of life.

Are some breeds naturally more intelligent?

Certain breeds are designed to evaluate situations more than others are. For instance, Border Collies, which are typically regarded as very intelligent dogs, are bred to herd sheep, so they need to watch those sheep, figure out where they are going, and head them off. This is something that wolves do naturally.

Every talent found in the dog came from the wolf. Wolves are herders, trackers, runners, and protectors. We have taken each of these talents, sharpened them, and selectively bred them into different kinds of dogs. So to say that certain breeds are more intelligent really isn't fair. Rather, each breed is intelligent in its own way, in the way it needs to be for its intended purpose. A Basset Hound is bred to follow a trail, nothing more. A Husky is bred to pull a sled and track polar bears. And a Shih Tzu is bred to be a cute little pet. A Border Collie wouldn't be able to track a polar bear, and a Husky wouldn't be able to herd sheep.

Why do large breeds like Great Danes die so young?

They die so young because dogs aren't supposed to be that big. The biggest wolf might weigh 100 pounds, but most wolves are much smaller. We have selectively bred some breeds of dog to be much larger, but the hearts of giant breeds must work much harder to supply their bodies with blood, so they will burn out faster. Their bones and joints must support more weight, which also makes them more susceptible to bone cancer and joint problems as they get older.

There is a genetic correlation between size, growth rates, and aging, but this connection is not yet completely understood. Large dogs age faster, and geneticists estimate that genes are responsible for 20-25 percent of the

variability noted in longevity. Big dogs may grow until they are two or three years old, but little dogs are often fully grown by six months of age. Growth hormones surging through the dog for a longer time will also speed up the aging process.

In nature, larger animals normally have longer life spans. But these animals evolved to be large in order to occupy a particular ecological niche. Their size occurred naturally to take advantage of a habitat or food source. Large dogs are the result of selective breeding rather than natural selection.

Are some breeds naturally neurotic?

Some breeds are more active, and these dogs may appear neurotic if they don't get as much exercise as they need. For example, a Parson Russell Terrier was bred to run around the barn all day, looking for rats and mice. If he is kept in an apartment, he will spend his days looking for imaginary vermin, and we might misinterpret this as neurosis. But this is just the breed's natural behavior. If this dog got more exercise, he would be happy to lie at your feet instead of chasing imaginary mice and rats.

Most "neurotic" behaviors seen in dogs are due to lack of exercise and activity. However, there are dogs that do have "loose wiring" in their brains. A real problem can be determined only by a veterinarian.

When I was a kid, all of the dogs on the block were outside all day long. In the summertime, you couldn't get down the block because it was full of kids and dogs from morning to night. It was fascinating to watch these dogs interact with one another. You would think they would have all stayed together in a pack, but that wasn't the case. Some of them formed cliques, while others did their own thing.

> ### WHISKERS
> Whiskers are sensors. When a dog comes into close contact with something, his whiskers will help him understand his environment, especially when he is in a situation where he can't see very well.

There was a Corgi named Dewey who was a roamer. He roamed the entire neighborhood in a very purposeful manner. He walked through backyards as if he were on his way to work. Another dog named Brady sat on her front lawn all day, chasing away the other dogs. My dogs stayed to themselves because I was working with them all day.

The idea of dogs staying in the house all day was unheard of. Of course, every now and then one got hit by a car, and we accepted that as a fact of life and got another dog. Dogs also had puppies. Some of the females were spayed, but no one castrated a male dog, and there was always someone who wanted the resulting puppies. A dog down the block named Mopsy bred with a neighbor's dog named Guy, and I remember looking at the puppies, wondering why some had long black hair and others had short white hair. This led to my interest in genetics.

Another interesting thing is that none of these dogs had behavior problems, chewed on their paws, or acted neurotic. They never chewed up things in the house or became nuisance barkers because they had things to do all day. Now, forty-five years later, when I go down that same block, the yards and streets are empty. There are no kids or dogs running loose. And the behavior of both kids and dogs has changed as a result. I'm not saying that we should let kids and dogs run loose as we did in the past, but we must compensate for the fact that neither gets that type of activity these days.

Are some breeds more likely than others to bite?

Some dogs are bred to be more protective and suspicious of strangers, so they may have the reputation of being more likely to bite. For example, today most guide dogs for the blind are Labrador Retrievers or Golden Retrievers, but when I was a kid most guide dogs were Airedale Terriers, Boxers, or German Shepherd Dogs. However, the public has a misconception about these latter breeds as untrustworthy. German Shepherds are used for police work, and when I was a kid we called them simply "police dogs" instead of German Shepherds. Many times, someone with compromised vision who had a German Shepherd as a guide dog would have trouble getting people to assist him because the people were afraid of the dog. But nobody is afraid of Labs and Goldens, which is why they are the breeds now most commonly used as guide dogs.

Misconceptions about various breeds are a result of the publicity they get. German Shepherds are used frequently in police work because of their versatility. But the breed also became known for its ability to chase criminals and bring them down. Drug dealers like pit bulls, especially pit bulls with poor temperaments. Traditionally, though, the pit bull was bred to fight other dogs but be very gentle with people. When I was a kid, Doberman Pinschers had the bad rap of the day. When you look at dog bite statistics, you need to remember that they are based on *reported* dog bites. If someone is bitten by his pet Toy Poodle, he is probably not going to report it. He will put a bandage on the bite and forget about it. If a Standard Poodle or a German Shepherd bites someone, that person is more likely to go to the hospital, and the bite will

PUPPY TEETH

Puppies get their first teeth when they are about three weeks old. Because they mature faster than humans do, they will start to get their adult teeth when they are four or five months old. Many people don't know that puppies lose their baby teeth because they never notice the baby teeth falling out. Puppy teeth are very tiny, and most of the time the puppy swallows them when they fall out.

be reported. So those statistics really don't mean anything. Popular breeds are also more likely to figure into dog bite statistics simply because there are more of these dogs. It doesn't mean that they are actually inflicting more dog bites.

In the nineteenth century, the Collie was considered a dangerous breed. It was also one of the most popular breeds. If a Collie bit someone, that person would probably go to the hospital. Boston Terriers were equally popular at that time. But if someone was bitten by a Boston Terrier, he probably would not end up going to the hospital.

A breed's reputation is a combination of public perception, the size of the dogs, and the relative percentage of responsible and irresponsible owners of that breed. Many small breeds also have a reputation for being nippy and prone to biting, but that's more likely a result of their owners' not training them to have self-control. The difference is that if a big dog snarls, people call the police, but if a little dog snarls, people think it's cute or funny. They film the dog and post the videos online.

Chihuahuas have a reputation for being nasty and aggressive. When I was a kid, all of the Chihuahuas I knew were owned by mean old ladies. They would carry their Chihuahuas around, and the dogs would just copy their owners' behavior. Good owners make good dogs, and bad owners make badly behaved dogs.

How do a dog's senses compare with those of a human?

Dogs win in terms of hearing and smell, but we have better senses of sight, taste, and touch.

Dogs inherited a keen sense of hearing from their wolf ancestors because it gave them a survival advantage. This legacy gives them the ability to detect faint sounds and high frequencies that are inaudible to humans. They are also much better at localizing sounds because their ears can move independently. Dogs can hear better and smell better than we can because these are the senses they need most to survive.

On the other hand, dogs don't need to see as well as we can; we can see in color because we need this to survive, but dogs do not. Any animal with primary colors as part of its makeup can see these colors, as they are part of the animal's communication system. For example, birds and fish can see the complete color spectrum, but dogs, cats, horses, mice, and rats have no primary colors in their makeup. Dogs can see certain colors like reds and browns, but they cannot see yellows or blues.

Do dogs shed every day?

All dogs shed, and they always shed more in the spring and fall. Normally, animals experience telogen (dormant) phases and anagen (active) phases during the hair growth cycle. During the anagen phase, hair grows rapidly. In nature, the anagen phase occurs in the spring and fall, forcing the old telogen hair out of the follicles. These phases are triggered by photoperiods. When there is more daylight in the spring, the follicles become active and the winter coat falls out as the summer coat grows in. In fall, there is less daylight, and the animal's summer coat falls out as the winter coat grows in.

You won't notice this as much if your dog lives mostly indoors. Indoor dogs shed more or less continuously, rather than lose a lot of coat within a few weeks, because they have less exposure to differing photoperiods. And after a while you get used to seeing dog hair on the furniture, so you don't notice it as much. Smaller dogs also shed less simply because less dog equals less hair to be shed. Shorthaired breeds like the Bulldog and Pug seem to shed more because the stiff hairs fall out more readily as they rub together. A lighter, curlier, or long-flowing coat will still shed, but the shedding is less noticeable for two reasons. First, the coat is more securely attached to the dog and the dead fur stays entangled in the coat until it is brushed or combed out. Second, dogs with these coat types usually go to a professional groomer more often.

BLUE EYES

Puppies' eyes are blue for the same reason that newborn Caucasian babies' eyes are blue. The blue-gray coloring protects the eyes until the puppy's nerves, muscles, and metabolism become fully functional. As the structures of the eyes mature, the irises of the eyes gradually clear to their true color, by four to six weeks of age.

Why do some dogs fart more than others do? How do you stop a dog from passing gas?

The reason for this is a combination of anatomy and diet. When dogs eat kibble, they tend to crunch their food much more. Dogs with loose lips and flat faces can swallow a lot of air this way. You can minimize a dog's gas problem by feeding a diet of canned food. Dogs consume softer foods in a more fluid motion and thus will take in less air in the process. If you cannot change your dog's diet for some reason, try feeding charcoal biscuits. The dog will still have a problem with gas, but it will be much less stinky. Excessive gas can also be the result of a food allergy, small intestine bacteria, or another type of intestinal problem.

Can Bulldogs and Pugs breathe as well as other dogs can?

Humans are attracted to brachycephalic breeds such as the Bulldog and Pug with their round heads, high foreheads, and flat faces—traits that are typically attributed to puppies. We find this look instinctively appealing, which also explains why young animals of social species look distinctly different from adults. This ensures that the adults will recognize them as young and will be protective of them, rather than treat them as adults or try to kill them. It doesn't always work, but it works most of the time. Brachycephalic breeds retain the puppylike look for their entire lives, which is technically known as neoteny.

When the brachycephalic look first appeared in dogs by accident, humans probably valued it and made a conscious effort to perpetuate it. Now we have several breeds—Pugs, Bulldogs, Boxers, to name a few—that fall into this category. These breeds have less tolerance to heat and can

have trouble breathing in hot weather. Their owners must be aware of this and exercise caution.

Flat-faced dogs can also have impaired breathing because of brachycephalic syndrome. These problems, such as pinched nostrils, stenotic nares, and overlong soft palate, can be corrected surgically.

How fast can a dog run? What breed is the fastest?

Sighthounds are the fastest breeds; they were genetically designed to be faster than wolves. The Greyhound is the fastest breed, and the fastest Greyhound has been clocked at 45 mph. The average dog can run about 19 mph, but this varies depending on the dog's overall size, physical condition, leg length, and whatever it happens to be chasing.

Why are some breeds clingy and others aloof?

Some breeds are genetically programmed to be more independent. For example, terriers were bred to live in the barn, not the house, and to use their own judgment when doing their job of ridding the barn of vermin. Beagles and Basset Hounds were bred to run ahead of the hunter and think for themselves when following an animal. On the other hand, English Setters and Cocker Spaniels were bred to wait until told by the hunter to go after a bird. They are programmed to follow and respond to humans. But the tendency toward independence varies among dogs within each breed. It is a very individual quality.

Why do some breeds bark more than others do?

Certain breeds have been selectively bred to bark to better perform their jobs. For instance, a hunting dog chasing a gazelle didn't need to bark. But if a human needs to follow along on the hunt, it helps if he can hear the dog barking. Barking also helps a herding dog turn the sheep. Barking is used

The Long and the Short of It

Children often ask me why some dogs have no tails and some have long tails. It's amazing that some people don't realize that certain breeds like Cocker Spaniels, Yorkshire Terriers, Poodles, and the different varieties of Schnauzer have their tails docked, or surgically shortened, usually a few days after birth. I've had many journalists call to ask my opinion on this procedure. Surgically changing a dog's anatomy is the quick way to change a dog's appearance. For instance, the screw tails found on Boston Terriers and Bulldogs are genetic. One dog happened to be born that way, people liked it, and they perpetuated it. Centuries ago, when different breeds were created, someone decided that certain breeds should have their tails shortened, and many reasons are given for this. Some say that breeds like Cocker Spaniels will have trouble if brambles and brush become stuck in their long tails. But there is always a contradiction. Why is it OK for a setter to have a long tail but a spaniel must have a short tail when they both are searching for birds in heavy cover?

What it really boils down to is human desire to have certain breeds look the way we want. I don't judge anyone for that. If the tail is docked soon after birth or the ears are cropped by a licensed veterinarian under anesthesia, I don't think it really bothers the dog. But it does bother some people. In Europe and England, it is illegal to crop a dog's ears or surgically shorten his tail. So, in Europe, Dobermans look something like Black and Tan Coonhounds, Great Danes have floppy ears, and Cocker Spaniels have long tails.

However, docking and cropping do cause some issues within breed clubs. Some people feel it is the dog's right to be left natural, while others feel that tradition should prevail. What I personally think will happen here in America is that we will eventually see separate classes at shows for breeds like Dobermans and Schnauzers so that they can be shown cropped and docked in one class and in their natural state in another, similar to the way that Dachshunds are shown in two size classes. This way, everyone's right as a pet keeper is respected.

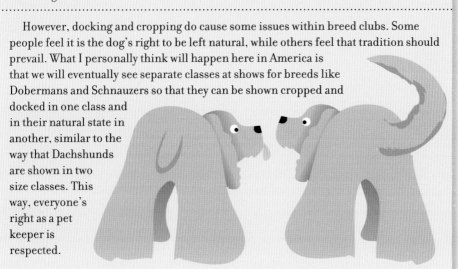

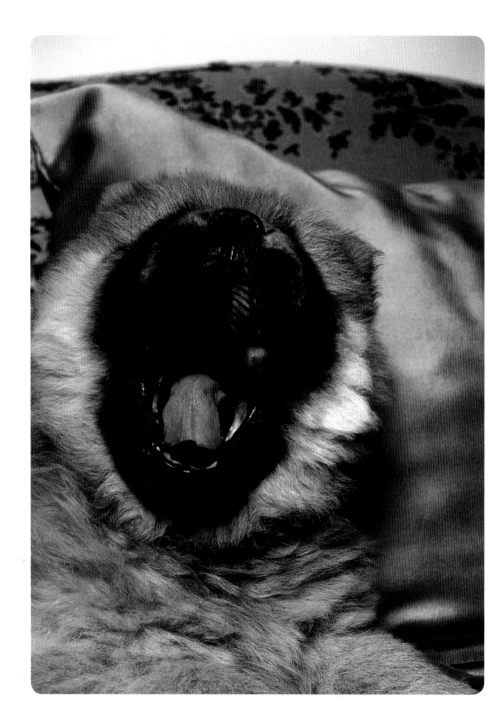

differently, or not at all, depending on the dog's job. Centuries later, the dog's original function still determines how much he will bark, even if that dog spends the whole day sitting around the house. Owners also add to the problem with unconscious training. When the dog barks, the owner pays attention, so the dog barks more.

Why do Chow Chows and Shar-Pei have blue-black tongues?

These unique breeds are from China, and obviously, way back when the Chinese were first breeding these dogs, one was born with a blue tongue. For whatever reason, the person who bred that dog liked that characteristic and kept the blue-tongued dog for future breeding. Therefore, the next generation also had the blue tongue trait. Many unusual traits in dogs began as a random mutations. If people like the random mutation, they breed the dog and thus pass the trait on. I can't tell you why someone liked the blue tongue, and, at this point, even the dogs don't know.

Can the New Guinea Singing Dog sing?

Wolves don't bark, and most primitive dogs bark very little. Wild canines usually howl or growl. The sound produced by the New Guinea Singing Dog is a combination of a howl, a yodel, and a growl all mixed together. It is one of the most primitive breeds, so it has not evolved to have the barking characteristic of more domesticated breeds.

DEPARTURES

Traveling with Your Dog

Random events are part of life, but proper care and husbandry must be part of your dog's life every day whether he is at home, on the road with you, or helping you out at work. Dogs have been traveling with people since the beginning of civilization. They have spread with us to every corner of the globe. However, traveling with their dogs causes a great deal of unnecessary grief and stress for many people.

My dogs travel with me all over, particularly when we are on TV. When I first started doing Martha Stewart's taped show ten years ago, they would travel with me in their carriers to her lovely studio in Westport, Connecticut. The studio was located on 3 acres of completely fenced property. As soon as we arrived, I would open the carriers, and the dogs would come tumbling out. They would run around the property for an hour. Knowing they could race around like lunatics in this safely enclosed area gave me a great sense of security and made my day of shooting much better. It also gave the dogs a chance to get all of the extra energy out of their systems, so they were nice and calm when it came time to shoot their specific parts of the show.

These days, Martha's show is done before a live audience in a Chelsea studio in New York City. And the dogs still can't figure out why it is different. Instead of racing around 3 acres of lawns and gardens, they sit next to me in the green room on their leashes. The only place they can run loose in the studio nowadays is in the freight elevator. But from their point of view, it's all fine as long as they are with me.

The point is that I am comfortable traveling with them and bringing them into different situations because I have done it so often. The first rule is to keep your dog in a crate when you travel. I learned this the hard way. One day, I was driving with my dog Barney, my best friend at the time. He was sitting on the front seat next to me. I stopped short and he went tumbling forward, hit the gearshift, and knocked the car into reverse, and we crashed into the car behind us. Fortunately,

no one was hurt, and the fact that the accident was caused by a dog brought a little levity to the situation for the poor guy behind me, who was minding his own business, just trying to get to work.

Since then, all of my dogs travel in crates. There are other ways to keep your dog safe and secure in the car, like seat belts and doggy car seats, but I believe that crates are best, especially for long-distance travel, because the dog can stretch out and sleep. We often traveled to Boston or Washington DC to tape shows, and six hours in a van with a dog can drive some people crazy. My dogs just sleep through the drive. They get a chance to stretch their legs when we come to a rest stop, which brings me to the second important rule of traveling. Always attach your dog's leash *before* you let him out of the car. And rule three is to have your dog microchipped before traveling with him.

One of my customers told me a terrible story about traveling to Florida with his family and their Dachshund. They were driving south on I-95 and stopped at a rest stop in Maryland. They opened the car, let the Dachshund out, blinked, and the Dachshund was gone. They looked everywhere, stayed overnight and searched the next day, and notified the police. Finally, with heavy hearts, they continued on their way to Florida with no Dachshund. Meanwhile, all the dog did was walk 30 feet to the other side of the rest stop and jump into somebody's car. These people assumed that someone had dumped the dog at the rest stop, and they took him home with them. Fortunately, these people picked the dog up and kept him safe. Unfortunately, they lived in Maine. When they got home, they took the dog to the vet. The vet looked at this well-cared-for Dachshund and thought that he looked like someone's pet. The vet had a microchip scanner, so he scanned the dog, read the chip number, and located the owners, who then had to drive from Florida to Maine to retrieve their dog.

How often should I bathe my dog? Is it a bad idea to bathe him too much?

Some people claim that bathing a dog too much will dry out his skin, but shampoo made for dogs is designed not to do that. So there is no harm in bathing a dog every day as long as you use the right shampoo, brush his coat out, and feed him a good diet containing enough fatty acids. Many show dogs are bathed at least weekly—sometimes even every day or more than once a day—and their coats look great. If your dog is dirty, wash him. I hate it when a dog gets dirty and stinky!

Which toys are safest for dogs? What if my dog swallows a toy?

Buy only toys made especially for dogs; do not offer your dog toys made for human children. Buy toys of the appropriate size and strength for your individual dog. However, even with these precautions taken, this does not mean that he cannot and will not destroy a toy that you give him. Where one dog might shred a latex squeaky toy and nibble on a little piece, another dog might swallow the squeaker or the entire toy.

This applies equally to toys that you buy and toys that you make. The jury is still out regarding the safety of homemade dog toys, but dogs have been creating their own toys out of our possessions for millennia. It does not matter whether we live in a cave or a fancy high-rise condo, they manage to do it somehow when left unsupervised with our possessions.

So what you need to do is determine what your dog likes to do when on his own. For instance, the Beagle in your dog may prefer to chew on things, and the terrier part of him may prefer to bite and shake. So if your dog is a chewer, then be sure that the cloth toy you make is hard enough and tight enough so that he cannot chew off chunks and swallow them. But the toy does need enough give to it so that the dog feels that there is some hope in chewing on it. Dogs rarely chew on rocks, as there is no point!

For a shaker-type toy, you need to be sure that there is enough length to it that the dog can grab one end and give it a good shake, while one end still has a big enough knot in it to give the toy some weight.

You have to use common sense. It has been my experience that if you think you will have a problem, then you probably will. Be proactive rather than reactive. The only way to ensure that a toy is safe is to know your dog and keep a close watch on him while he plays with it. If he is inclined to swallow things, it is very possible that he could swallow a toy. It is your responsibility as a pet keeper to know these things and take precautions as needed.

Is rawhide bad for my dog? Are some kinds of rawhide better than others?

There are two problems with rawhide. The first is the chemicals used to cure it, although these days many manufacturers make rawhide that is chemical and preservative free. The second problem occurs when dogs break off chunks of rawhide and swallow them. These big pieces can't be digested and can cause a dangerous obstruction. Swallowing a small piece of rawhide won't hurt your dog, but rawhide gets mushy as the dog chews, and it is easy for large pieces to be ingested. It is your responsibility as a pet keeper to pay attention to anything your dog chews, whether a rawhide, an edible chew bone, a rubber toy, or a stuffed toy. Swallowing chunks of anything can be dangerous.

How do I keep my dog from digging up my flower beds?

If you watched your dog 24/7 and stopped him every time he tried to dig, you wouldn't have any problem. But when he is outside in the yard unsupervised, at some point he will probably start thinking what fun it would be to dig up the nice soft flower beds.

I solved the digging problem by putting chicken wire over my flower beds, pegging it down with wire coat hangers to hold it in place, cutting holes for the plants, and covering everything with a layer of mulch. If you want a more contemporary look, you can cover it with gravel. If you already have plants, just cut holes for them when you put the chicken wire down. This method will also stop stray cats from pooping in your flower beds.

At first, the dogs tried to dig through the wire. They sniffed and investigated and figured out that the chicken wire was covering the entire flower bed, so there was no point in digging there. I made them a spot in one corner of the yard that was filled with play sand in which I buried treats for them. They made their own decision about where they wanted to dig.

What's the largest litter possible for a dog?

I just read about a Bull Terrier that had a litter of fourteen. I'm sure this isn't the biggest litter, but it is the biggest one to make news recently. The dog in *101 Dalmatians* had twenty-one puppies, and perhaps that number was chosen based on an actual incident that the author heard about at the time she was writing the book. I've wondered why the author chose the number twenty-one. There are no facts and figures to back it up. Information on most of the very large litters that make the news is purely anecdotal. Some breeds, like Huskies and pit bulls, are known for large litters, but the average litter size seems to be five to eight puppies.

Why do big dogs have big litters and small dogs have small litters?

This is directly related to the volume of the uterus. A big uterus can hold more puppies. Today, tiny dogs are popular, and everyone wonders why they cost so much. This is partly because small dogs have only a few puppies at a time.

Are there any small breeds that have big litters?

Some smaller breeds that have longer bodies, like Dachshunds, can have larger litters. A short-backed Pomeranian will only have one or two pups, but a Dachshund can have five or six, which is a big litter for a dog that size.

At what age is it safe to take a puppy away from his mother?

Puppies can be weaned at five or six weeks old, and even though a puppy is physically able to leave his mother at that age, his mental and psychological development won't tolerate it. The longer that the puppy stays with his mother and siblings, the more socialized he will be. The mother teaches the puppy appropriate play and social skills that can't be learned from humans. Most

breeders recommend that puppies stay with their mothers for at least eight or nine weeks, and it is against the law to transport puppies younger than eight weeks old.

Very often, dogs that are separated from their mothers too soon are the dogs that tend to develop psychological problems because they didn't have a chance to socialize with other dogs during those early critical weeks.

Why doesn't the father dog help raise the puppies?

In nature, all male wild canids help raise their puppies because it is to their advantage to stay with their mates and ensure that their puppies grow up. Those puppies are carrying the males' genes.

Also in the wild, it is too hard for a mother fox or wolf to raise puppies on her own. For domesticated dogs, this isn't the case. Humans have helped with the job of puppy raising for so many generations that as time went by, male dogs lost the instinct to help their mates because it wasn't necessary anymore.

In a state of nature, if a male wasn't a good father, his puppies were less likely to survive. Therefore, males that were good fathers produced more

puppies that survived to perpetuate this gene. When humans started getting involved in the process, they took over much of the male's role. The offspring of all males survived, regardless of whether the males had the instinct to help raise the puppies. It was no longer a survival issue. As the generations progressed, this instinct was bred out of dogs. It doesn't mean that a male dog is not as nice as a male wolf. It's just that the male wolf has to help raise the youngsters to ensure that his genes are passed on. Humans will make sure that a dog's genes are passed on.

How often do female dogs come into season? How long does it normally last?

Domestic dogs—except for the primitive Basenji and Dingo—come into season every six months. The primitive breeds come into season only once a year. The cycle usually lasts for three weeks, one week coming in, one week to be bred, and one week going out. But male dogs will be attracted to a female for the whole three weeks, sometimes even longer.

How do sex-related characteristics factor into my selection of a dog?

Males tend to be a little larger, with heads that are a little wider, but that is about the only generalization you can make about differences between the sexes. There is no truth to the idea that one sex is friendlier, more aggressive, or easier to train.

My most intense emotional relationships have always been with male dogs, but that is just my personal experience. I've had three or four dogs that could practically read my mind, and they were all males. That doesn't mean you can't have a close relationship with a female dog, of course.

Small females can be more easily trained to use wee-wee pads, but males can also be trained to do this. If you want to train a dog to squat and urinate on a wee-wee pad, this is most likely going to be a small dog. Larger dogs of either sex are usually trained to go outside because of the volume of urine they produce. If you want to train a male dog to use a wee-wee pad, the process is less complicated if he is neutered before his testosterone kicks in at six to nine months of age. This way, he never gets into the habit of lifting his leg to urinate against an object.

Is it OK to let my puppy sleep in bed with me?

That depends on who else is in bed with you. Personally, I could not do this because I have too many dogs, and it wouldn't be fair to let only one sleep in the bed. If you don't mind having the dog in your bed for his entire life, there is nothing wrong with it. But it won't be easy to train him not to sleep in the bed if you decide after five years of allowing it that you don't want him to do it anymore.

From the standpoint of house-training, this really isn't an issue. If the puppy is in the bed and he wakes up, you will wake up, too, and can take him outside. All in all, it is a lifestyle choice more than anything else.

Is it safe to travel with/ship my dog on an airplane?

I ship dogs all over the world, from Kenya to Japan to Iceland. Many companies that relocate their business executives pay me to send over their dogs. This is typically very safe. Once in a while there will be a problem, such as a dog getting loose at the airport. These incidents make the news, but you never hear about the millions of animals that are shipped without incident. Of course, the dog's safety and comfort depend on the shipper's doing things the right way and adhering to the following rules:

- The dog must travel in a secure airline-approved kennel.
- The crate should be lined with a thick layer of shredded paper to soak up any moisture.
- A water bottle should be affixed to the door of the crate.
- A bag of food should be attached to the outside of the crate and a dish attached to the inside of the door so that food can be put into the dish without opening the crate. These dishes come with little hooks to attach them to the door, but I always drill a little hole in the dish so I can secure it to the door with a zip tie. This prevents the dog from knocking or pulling the dish off the door during the flight.
- The crate door must be securely locked, with nylon zip ties added for extra security.
- Direct flights should be used if possible.
- Major airlines should be used; look for those that provide a pet safety program in case flights are delayed or canceled.

- Dogs should travel on nighttime flights if possible to avoid the hottest part of the day. Further, some breeds are restricted from travel during summer months.

These are the rules for most dogs. If traveling with their owners, the smallest of dogs are permitted in the cabin if their crates fit under the seats. Ninety-nine percent of air-travel and shipping problems are avoidable if you are careful and plan properly. Call the airline first and make sure that you know what it requires, which will include a health certificate and vaccination record from the veterinarian. And never, ever ship a dog that has been tranquilized. Actually, according to the International Air Transport Association (IATA), it is illegal for tranquilized animals to be shipped.

My worst shipping experience happened when I shipped a dog from JFK Airport in New York to Valencia, Spain. Unfortunately, we could not use any Spanish airlines because they were on strike. We shipped on Lufthansa from New York to Frankfurt, where the dog had a two-hour layover before the final leg of the trip to Valencia. However, there was an engine problem with the second flight, and it was canceled. Lufthansa scheduled this particular flight only once a week, but the people at Lufthansa had an extremely good kenneling situation in Frankfurt, and the dog was fine there for six days until we were able to get him on the next flight.

Should my dog wear booties in the winter? Should he wear a coat?

Throughout history, dogs have adapted to whatever climates they lived in. However, it wasn't common for Huskies to live in Florida or for a Mexican Hairless to live in Alaska. Dogs don't choose where they live; their owners have to help them acclimate. In cold weather, shorthaired dogs will appreciate a coat. Dogs that walk on city streets in winter will appreciate protection from the salt, slush, and ice. Eskimos also put booties on their dogs to protect them from the elements.

Whatever you put on your dog, make sure it is comfortable for him. With booties, put them on the dog and let him practice walking in the house before you go outside. Let him become familiar with the sensation of wearing them so that he's not overwhelmed. If you take the time to make the unfamiliar familiar to the dog, he will have no issues.

Why do so many beaches and parks in America ban dogs?

This is mainly a result of irresponsible dog owners. If you let your dog run wild and terrorize people or you let him poop in public areas and don't clean it up, you ruin it for responsible dog owners. Not everyone likes dogs as much as we do. And we have to respect the wishes of the majority. You can't fight city hall. If you bring your dog to a park where dogs are allowed, please be responsible and don't let him do anything to offend people who don't like dogs.

Are dog shows "beauty contests"?

No, they're not. In a human beauty contest, the appearance of the contestants is determined by the random mixing of their genes. The women are either beautiful or not beautiful, and it has nothing to do with deliberate breeding.

A dog show encompasses much more. The appearance of dog-show entries is being evaluated based on selective breeding for very specific traits that must stay consistent within the different breeds. Each particular breed must conform to an official standard as set forth by the respective breed club. A purebred dog's appearance reflects his purpose, or a particular culture, or a time in human history. I would compare dog shows to history lessons rather than beauty contests.

Should I register my dog with the American Kennel Club?

The American Kennel Club (AKC) is what's called a breed registry. It's just a club, like the Elks Club, Lion's Club, or Kiwanis Club. Anybody with an eligible purebred dog can get the dog registered with the AKC. It is definitely the oldest and most prestigious breed registry. The AKC has the most rules, and some people do not agree with these rules. Therefore, other dog fanciers created their own clubs. There are other breed-registry associations out there, like the United Kennel Club, the American Canine Association, and the American Rare Breed Association. Each organization has its own set of rules, and I am not saying that any one club's rules are right or wrong. It is a free country, and anyone is entitled to register his dog with the club that he prefers.

SUNBURNS
Many white breeds have very sensitive skin, and they can get sunburned. Human sunblocks can work well for dogs, but you must make sure that your dog can lick the sunscreen with no ill effects. Ask your vet to recommend a safe product.

Do you recommend invisible fences for suburban dogs?

Invisible fencing can work very well, but I would never use one as a perimeter fence for my property. If my dog saw a rabbit on the other side of the fence, he would take off and burst right through the barrier, regardless of a shock deterrent. And once he was through the fence, it would be unlikely for him to come back into the yard if it meant getting another shock. An invisible fence also provides no way to stop other dogs and animals from coming onto your property. They won't be wearing the collars and radio attachments, so they can wander right into your yard with no adverse effects.

Invisible fences are best for keeping your dogs out of certain areas of your own property. You should still have a wood or chain-link fence around the yard's perimeter for security.

Why Dog People Are the Most Important People on the Planet

There are two types of people: those who like dogs and those who don't. And the people who don't like dogs enjoy making fun of dog people. What they don't realize is that their entire civilization can be traced back to us dog people.

People started training wolves 20,000 years ago. They had no idea that a wolf could eventually become a dog, and they had no idea how important a dog could be. A few people were fascinated by wolves, but most people saw them as predators and competition. If some wolves started hanging around the human campsites, most people threw rocks at them. Regardless of precisely how domestication came about, at some point an early human looked at a wolf and saw something other than a predator or a fur coat. These people were early pet keepers, most likely the ancestors of you and me! Instead of trying to drive the wolves away, they studied them and tried to make friends with them. And most likely these people were laughed at, just as I was because I liked animals. But once this early man made friends with the wolf, he had a real advantage when there wasn't enough food in the winter.

Let's assume that the early pet keeper brought along his tame wolf when he went off to hunt with the rest of the tribe. Now, let's say that someone saw a deer and threw a spear at it, but the injured deer ran off and the person couldn't follow it. The wolf could track that deer, bring it down, and kill it. As a result, the people had food that day. If that happened often enough, the advantage of having a tame wolf would become obvious.

As a result of hunting with that tame wolf, people found themselves with plenty of food and more free time to do things like create artwork on the cave walls and other technological innovations. This also produced a shift in thinking. Rather than thinking about what the animals could do for them dead, the people started realizing that animals might be able to do a lot for them when they were alive.

Domesticated animals have enabled man to thrive and reproduce to the obscene numbers that we have today. Without the early pet keepers who wanted to learn about animals, none of this would have happened. Of course, the earth might be a more pristine place if this had never happened.

Should I give my dog a short haircut in the summer?

I've often read that it's not a good idea to do this because long hair serves as insulation for the dog. Insulation not only keeps out cold but also helps deflect heat away from the dog's body surface. It is much like the long, flowing robes worn by Bedouin nomads to protect them from the heat and sun in the deserts of the Middle East. But I have noticed that wild canines living in hot areas such as Israel, India, and Portugal have very short coats. Wolves and wild dogs in northern areas have longer, heavier coats in winter and shorter coats in summer. This is natural for a wild canine, but the length of a domesticated dog's coat is determined by selective breeding. An Old English Sheepdog will have a long coat year-round. I do believe that dogs with long or heavy coats are much more comfortable with shorter coats in hot weather.

You have to be careful if you shave a dog that has pale skin. Don't cut the coat too short, or the dog might suffer from sunburn. This varies, as some dogs have darker skin than others. Dark-colored dogs usually have a higher concentration of melanin in their skin, which provides more protection against sunburn.

Let's Get Together

About ten years ago, I started doing a local cable TV show about pet care. The hour-long show was live and had no commercials. It was just me in an old studio, answering questions for people about their pets. When I had originally talked to the producers, they asked me to bring a dog and just answer questions. But I felt like a jerk just standing there for an hour with my bird Harry on my shoulder and my dog Barney next to me, especially because I never knew what to do with my hands. I was on live TV, on a set. A newscaster has papers to shuffle. A person who is giving a lecture is behind a podium. But I was just standing there on live TV for an hour.

For Cablevision, this show was at the bottom of the list. It was a very low-budget production, and they had no funds to do anything with the set. So I started bringing in as many of my pets as I could. At first I would keep the cats in a basket, the bunny rabbits in another basket, and the birds on a perch. At least I was able to touch them and play with them, so I felt more comfortable. This went on for quite some time.

One day, in the middle of winter, I arrived to do the show and found that there was no heat in the studio. Even though the lights were very bright, they didn't generate enough heat to warm up the studio. I was freezing, and the animals were freezing. We were all freezing for an hour on live TV. Eventually, I realized that the rabbits, cats, and dogs were all clumping together to try to keep warm. I kept pulling them apart and they kept clumping together to get warm. Whatever inhibitions they had about one another fell by the wayside because they were so cold. It was a matter of survival.

The next day, I got faxes and phone calls from people telling me how much they enjoyed watching the animals interact with one another. (E-mail was not the norm in those days, and what a nice time that was. These days, my life is overrun with e-mail. I am probably one of the few people who doesn't own a BlackBerry and never will. Every e-mail I have to answer takes time away from my pets.)

I realized that I had enjoyed the show, the animals had enjoyed it, and the audience had enjoyed it. After that, I started picking and choosing animals that would interact with one another for the show. Choosing animals that would get along helped offset the incongruity of the whole situation. We never did have any sets for this show. My animals became the sets simply because I have so many. Some of them really came to enjoy doing this.

Critics of mine complained that people would see all of these animals together and try to replicate the same thing at home. Someone would try to get his cat to hang out with his bird, and the bird would be eaten. But in reality, what was happening to me on television was also happening to people at home. They were watching the show with their dogs and cats on their couches, their birds on perches, and maybe rabbits in cages on the floor. We keep all of these domesticated animals, and they do have the ability to get along. But to keep my critics at bay, I put a disclaimer at the end of my show stating that all of the animals were specially trained by me to get along and that viewers should not try this at home. But none of the animals were ever trained for this. Either they got along, or I didn't bring them on TV. If you have many pets, you always have a variety to choose from for situations like this.

What is the best dog for kids?

I get this question a lot, and the answer is simple: the best dog for kids is whatever the parents want to take care of. Kids have gotten along with all kinds of dogs for thousands of years. If a kid wanted to hurt a dog, he would be able to hurt a dog of any size.

In general, smaller dogs with short hair are less work. Whatever type of dog you choose should complement, rather than complicate, your family's lifestyle. But I really can't make these judgment calls for other people.

Years ago, a woman contacted me to help her find a Golden Retriever puppy. She had five small children and was expecting her sixth. I thought that the last thing she needed was a puppy, but she was insistent, so I helped her find a puppy. Six months later, she came to see me with her puppy and her six children, wanting me to help her find another Golden puppy. I really thought this was a bad idea, but her first puppy was so well trained, happy, and well behaved that I agreed. Three years later, I heard from her again, and she was ready to get her third Golden.

I knew another lady who got a Golden puppy when she was eighty-five, and she had the dog until she was ninety-five. They both aged gracefully together. She died at ninety-five, and the dog went to her daughter. Those experiences taught me not to be judgmental. You are the best judge of what type of dog will or will not fit into your lifestyle.

One thing I do recommend for busy parents is to consider getting an older dog. Forget about getting a puppy; go to a shelter or rescue group and adopt

Piro the Puppy

My first dog was a little black mixed-breed puppy that my grandfather got for me when I was five years old. He didn't ask my parents first—he just wanted to score "Grandpa points," so he went to the shelter on Christmas Eve and got me this little puppy. Of course, I was entranced by him; the only pet I had had up to that point was a pigeon. Unfortunately, my parents are not animal people, and at age five my pet-keeping abilities were limited. My parents couldn't handle the responsibility, so they took the puppy back to the shelter a week later. This broke my heart, but I couldn't take care of him and Grandpa wasn't helping. I never forgot him. That's why to this day whenever I'm asked about the best dog for children, I always say that the best dog is whatever the parents want to take care of.

an older dog. The shelter can tell you which dogs would be good with kids. The first year of raising a puppy is the most difficult. An older dog will need some time to adjust to your home, but he likely will already be house-trained and know some basic commands. And you also know what you are getting in terms of size, coat, and personality. This is a real advantage if your lifestyle cannot accommodate a lot of surprises.

Why do some dogs dislike men?

Dogs don't instinctively dislike men or women; they dislike certain people, namely people who violate their territory. Most of the time, this happens to be a man in a uniform, like a mailman or a delivery man. All of these people regularly enter the dog's territory simply to do their job, but that's not how the dog sees it. My dogs dislike anyone in a uniform; they bark and carry on when delivery people arrive every day. Delivery people also generally walk in a purposeful manner, which promotes animosity. Since you typically see more delivery men than delivery women, and because men typically move in a more purposeful manner, it's easy to start thinking that some dogs just dislike men.

My two dogs used to get along great, but they have started fighting, and it seems to be getting worse. What can I do?

There are all kinds of reasons why dogs fight; sometimes they get along, and sometimes they don't. Some experts say that the best combination is a male and a female, but I've seen fights between opposite-sex dogs too. I've also heard that fights between two females tend to be worse, but I've seen some bad fights between males.

If they have teeth and a personality, there can sometimes be conflict. The key is to see what is triggering the conflict. Dog pairs are like human pairs. Sometimes we disagree, but then everything's fine. Then something occurs, maybe an argument about time or money, and you have another conflict. If we had someone watching over us all the time who stepped in to remove every source of conflict, we wouldn't fight. That's what you have to do with your dogs.

Watch your dogs carefully and learn what triggers the problem—food, a toy, your attention. You as pet keeper must find and remove that trigger from the relationship. If it's food, feed the dogs in separate rooms. If there are toys

Dogs and New Babies

You often hear advice about showing your dog a doll or bringing home a baby blanket from the hospital to help him understand that a new baby is coming. But in real life, I doubt that any of these things work. When you show a doll to your dog, he knows that it's not a real person. Giving him a blanket with the baby's smell on it isn't going to make a big impression on the dog either. You come home with different smells on you every day, and that doesn't mean much to the dog at all.

But dogs do know people, and most—not all—dogs have an instinctive liking for children because wolves are instinctively protective toward wolf cubs. The key is to supervise all interactions between the dog and the baby. When you bring the baby home from the hospital, hold the dog and the baby securely, and allow the dog to satisfy his curiosity and sniff the baby.

However, before the baby comes home from the hospital, it's a very good idea to reinforce your dog's basic obedience training. If you are carrying a baby, you don't want the dog jumping on you. You want him to sit and lie down strictly on voice commands. It's never going to work if the dog is jumping all over you while you are trying to get into the house with the baby and a bag of groceries. So making sure that your dog is well versed in his commands is the most important thing you can do to prepare him for the arrival of a new baby.

Remember to never let your child interact with the dog unless you supervise, and be sure your child grows up respecting the dog. When my son was little, I allowed him to run wild all over my dogs. He would jump on them, grab their ears, and pull their tongues out of their mouths, and the dogs tolerated this. In my stupidity, I thought this was a reflection of my abilities as a pet keeper. My dogs were so tolerant toward children that they would never object to this sort of interaction. But I created a monster, because as my son grew up, he thought he could do these things to every dog he saw. He had no second thoughts about walking up to a strange dog and grabbing his ears or tail. So I had to backtrack and teach a one-year-old to "be nice to the doggies." If I had done this from the get-go, he would have only approached dogs respectfully. It's always better to be proactive than reactive.

lying around, pick them up and give one toy to each dog in separate spots. If the dogs fight when you greet them, change how you greet them. Dogs often get excited and may bump into each other as they try to get close to you. Their proximity to each other and high levels of emotion may cause them to lash out at each other. Instead of greeting them when you walk through the door, get them out into the yard as soon as you come home so they have plenty of room to bounce around and carry on.

In certain situations, some dogs may really fight with each other. There is a difference between dogs not getting along and dogs hurting each other. In the latter case, you must be prepared to keep the dogs separated in the house using crates, gates, or whatever it takes. It's not a pleasant situation and there is no quick fix, but sometimes it is the only way to keep them safe.

Is it a good idea to get a new dog to keep my old dog company?

What you have to realize is that the old dog is not pining away for another dog to play with. If he has never had that experience, he isn't automatically going to feel that something is missing from his life. Some old dogs may not want a new dog around because they want to sleep all day, but I personally feel that most dogs like the company of other dogs. An old dog may not like a puppy jumping on him all day, but the puppy will be spending time in his crate for training and can be separated from the older dog at other times when the dog needs his peace. The benefits are that the older dog has another dog to compare notes with, compare smells with. I really think dogs like to have other dogs to communicate with.

Imagine if you lived in a beautiful alien spaceship, and it was just you and the aliens. The aliens treated you really well, and you could understand a little of what they said, but you couldn't talk to them. You would long for someone who could understand you, and this is also true of singly-kept dogs. They are happy and accepting of their situation, but they would appreciate having another dog to talk to.

We want to adopt a dog from the animal shelter. Can you give me some tips on how to choose the right one?

The best way to choose a dog for adoption is to take the advice of the people working at the shelter. There is a special place in heaven for people who work in shelters. It can be a horrible job sometimes. It is very depressing to hear all of the excuses that people make when they drop their dogs off at the shelter just because they don't want to take care of them anymore.

In a good animal shelter, the shelter workers know their animals very well. They do temperament testing, and they have the skills to make good matches between dogs and families. Take your family to the shelter, meet the people who work with the dogs, and describe what type of dog you are looking for. They will be able to help you choose a dog to complement, rather than complicate, your life. The last thing they want is for a dog to end up back in the shelter, so they are very motivated to make a good match and ensure that once you take a dog home with you, he will stay there.

Some very busy municipal shelters don't have the resources to temperament-test their dogs before adoption. That makes for a trickier situation. Many shelters and rescues do temperament-test their dogs, and they will let you know about this. That's why dogs are classified as being "good with children" or "not good with cats" or "dog aggressive." If a shelter doesn't have the funds or manpower to do this, you have to be more careful about choosing a dog. If you feel uncomfortable about taking a dog home or the workers don't give you the answers you want to hear, don't take the dog. Go to another shelter, do more

> ### SIZE MATTERS
> Small dogs like Chihuahuas have more fun playing with other Chihuahuas simply because it is easier for them to play with dogs their own size. They will prefer this if given a choice. Dogs don't have any idea of their breed; all dogs think of themselves as equal to other dogs. But they will recognize dogs that belong to their own pack, which is often more dogs of the same breed.

research, or go to a reliable breeder who can better advise you about a dog's temperament.

My new puppy doesn't like my husband. What do I do?

Well, new puppies really can't like or dislike anybody. The puppy may be scared of your husband. Perhaps your husband may be bigger, louder, or more confident than anyone the puppy has met so far. Because of this, the puppy may feel shy around him and more comfortable around you and other family members.

You can't tell the puppy that your husband is a nice person. It's a matter of your husband spending more quality time with the puppy and you spending a little less time with the puppy. Only the puppy can decide that he is comfortable around your husband, and that won't happen unless the puppy spends time with him.

My dog and cat want nothing to do with each other. How can I get them to be friends?

You may not be able to get them to be friends, but you can still get them to coexist. Dogs and cats have been cohabitating since early human civilization. They rode in reed canoes with early Polynesian sailors. They rode in covered wagons together from the East Coast to the West Coast. Wherever people have gone, they have taken their dogs and cats with them, and the dogs and cats have not killed each other.

The key is for the dog to realize that the cat is not something to be chased and tortured; this may be something you have to teach your dog. Once the cat realizes that the dog is not going to hurt her, she will be confident. What I do is let the cat stay in a separate room if she wants to. I will bring the dog into the room on a leash and just sit there for an hour, reading a book. The dog is on a leash, and the cat is hiding under the bed. They are well aware of each other's presence in the room. We do this every day. As time goes on, the cat gradually realizes that the dog is not going to hurt her, and she becomes much more confident. But this can happen only if they spend time together in a nonconfrontational setting. Only you can provide this type of setting. If the animals are just running wild in the house, the dog will continue chasing the cat, and one of them will eventually get hurt.

My dog Buddy has an extremely strong prey drive. This can cause a lot of problems when you have a lot of free-roaming cranes, pheasants, and chickens in the backyard, as I do. I would sit in a chair in the backyard with Buddy on a retractable leash. He would go to the end of the leash and check out the birds, and I would constantly call him back to me and give him a treat. After doing this for months, Buddy began to ignore the birds. He could not act on his desire to chase them and kill them, so while he did not develop affection for the birds, he simply started to ignore them. Now, since they are no longer prey,

My Chihuahua, Murphy the Terror

Murphy was given to me by someone from the local humane society. She called me to say that she had a perfect Chihuahua mix for me in her shelter. He would be perfect for my TV show because he is such a ham, but he is also a little monster. And that's why he ended up in the shelter. He doesn't like to have his nails trimmed; he doesn't like baths. He is a dog that bites first and thinks about it later, and this attitude hasn't changed in the ten years that I've had him.

I have developed ways to work around this. I keep him away from people I know he is going to bite, and I muzzle him when I cut his nails. I accept Murphy for what he is, but I am a responsible pet keeper, and I make sure that he doesn't get a chance to bite anyone.

He is the best TV dog I've ever had. He knows exactly where to stand and what to do. It's well worth the extra management I have to deal with. Some people say it's just a dominance issue, and they ask me how I can let a 5-pound dog dominate me. That has nothing to do with it. Obviously, I could take on Murphy, but why would I want to do that and break his spirit? I would rather just accept his limitations and work around them.

they have no relevance to him whatsoever. Likewise, the birds stopped acting afraid of Buddy, so they no longer elicited his prey drive. The same principle applies to my cats. Buddy does not like them or play with them the way my other dogs do. He totally ignores them, and that's all I ask.

I will add that I have owned many wolves and wolf hybrids, and I have never been able to erase the prey drive in those animals. They instinctively classify all other animals as either food or nonfood, and I have found it impossible to revise this response in nondomesticated canines.

Is it safe to let my dog play with my bird?

My dogs get along fine with birds, but this is not so much a play situation. Generally, a pet bird does not act afraid of dogs, so its behavior does not trigger a dog's prey drive. If the same bird were fluttering madly across the floor, the dog might react quite differently.

My Cairn Terrier Buddy, who has an extremely strong prey drive, got along with a little tiny chicken one-tenth his size who wasn't afraid of him. Buddy chased every other chicken, but because this one walked right up to him and didn't try to run, he didn't bother trying to chase her. She even made a nest in his dog run. Maybe she thought she was safe there. I don't think he thought of her as a friend or something to play with, but he certainly didn't recognize her as prey.

In situations like this, though, the bird is at the dog's mercy. So you as the pet keeper have the responsibility to supervise and to make sure that the bird is not going to get hurt.

Can dogs be homosexual?

Dogs will mount other dogs of the same sex, but animals can't have true homosexual bonds because it would be an evolutionary dead end. A pair of same-sex animals would not be able to perpetuate their species, which is a biological imperative. Dogs are opportunists, and if they can have sex with another dog, a pillow, or your leg, that is fine with them. True homosexual behavior is characterized by a much narrower preference.

Which breeds get along best with cats?

As a general rule, dogs that were not bred to hunt small animals have a lower prey drive; for example, a Saint Bernard may get along better with

The Story of Barney and Calvin

One of my favorite dogs was a mixed breed named Barney. My wife and I had just gotten married, and we wanted another dog. We went to the shelter, and she really liked this dog that looked like a small Golden Retriever. The card said that his name was Barney. He sat down and offered her his paw, so we had to take him.

However, Barney was in the shelter for a good reason. He had some kind of chronic immune-deficiency syndrome that caused a lot of soft-tissue problems, leading to chronic diarrhea and gingivitis. I made my vet very rich during the first year we had Barney.

He was a very effeminate-looking dog, and I never thought much about this until one night when I was walking him. A neighbor's pit bull got loose and came barreling toward us and jumped on Barney. To my surprise, Barney gave that dog such a thrashing that the pit bull ran away screaming.

Later, I got a Bull Terrier puppy named Calvin, and it became Barney's mission in life to keep Calvin thrashed and trashed. Barney beat him up every day, and Calvin, in his good-natured Bull Terrier way, didn't care.

Some time later, my friend Robert wanted to keep Calvin for a while. My son had just been born and we had a lot on our minds, so Calvin went to live with him for six months. Barney and Calvin didn't see each other at all during that time until the day Robert brought Calvin back. Calvin stuck his nose into the 2-inch space between my fence and gate, and suddenly Barney realized he was back and promptly bit him on the nose. Calvin let out a roar. Not a growl or a snarl, but a roar, and he started slamming himself against the gate. Barney realized that he had gone a little too far that time. At that point, we knew that Barney and Calvin would never get along, so he still lives with Robert.

Calvin is also a cancer survivor. He developed lymphoma seven years ago and went through a very expensive round of chemotherapy. He is fine today, but he still hates Barney. If he had a picture of Barney on the wall, he would be throwing darts at it.

small animals than a Dachshund will. However, plenty of Dachshunds get along fine with cats, hamsters, and guinea pigs. I have owned a Dachshund named Dixie for twelve years now, and she gets along fine with small animals. The best way to make this determination is to look at the breed's original purpose. You can research this easily by going to www.akc.org and clicking on each breed's history. A Shih Tzu was bred to be a cute little pet. A Havanese was bred to be a cute little pet. A Parson Russell Terrier was bred to hunt creatures like foxes, rats, and badgers.

Huskies also have a strong prey drive. When they were not pulling sleds, the Inuit people used them to track seals and polar bears. Breeders who created the Cavalier King Charles Spaniel or the Japanese Chin didn't care if they had a drive to chase small animals. That was never their intended purpose. Their prey drive was reduced because no one intentionally enhanced it through selective breeding. Breeds like coonhounds and Beagles were used to chase small animals, so they obviously have a stronger prey drive. Of course, nothing is written in stone. Regardless of breed, some dogs have more natural prey drive than others do. I personally have never encountered a dog that I could not desensitize to cats, rabbits, or any other small animal.

I would say that just about any individual dog has the capability to learn that certain animals are meant to be chased and others are not. They key is to prevent the dog from having opportunities to act on his desire to chase cats. And the cat must likewise lose her fear of the dog through consistent, uneventful associations.